SAL SALVADOR'S
SINGLE STRING STUDIES
FOR GUITAR

UPDATED EDITION WITH TAB

BY
SAL SALVADOR

EDITED BY
BOB GRILLO

BIOGRAPHIES PROVIDED BY
LORINDA R. SMIRAGLIA

ISBN 978-1-4950-5760-1

HAL•LEONARD®
CORPORATION
7777 W. BLUEMOUND RD. P.O. BOX 13819 MILWAUKEE, WI 53213

In Australia Contact:
Hal Leonard Australia Pty. Ltd.
4 Lentara Court
Cheltenham, Victoria, 3192 Australia
Email: ausadmin@halleonard.com.au

Visit Hal Leonard Online at
www.halleonard.com

ABOUT SAL SALVADOR

Sal Salvador, a versatile self-taught guitarist, built a career that encompassed performing, recording, and extensive contributions to music education. Often called a "musician's guitarist" and an enthusiastic music explorer, he was also a contributor to the bebop revolution. He played challenging solos inventively, yet always remained melodic, warm-toned and lyrical.

Sal became fascinated with the jazz guitar as a teenager after hearing Charlie Christian records. His formative years were spent practicing eight hours a day, taking correspondence courses and asking questions of local professionals. He started playing in jazz groups in Springfield, Mass. with aspiring musician friends, saxophonist Phil Woods and drummer Joe Morello.

In the late 1940s on the advice of Tommy Dorsey, Sal went to New York equipped with only six dollars and a guitar, determined to take his career to the next level. He roomed with Tal Farlow, Jimmy Raney, and hometown friend Phil Woods. He studied music theory with Harry Volpe and booked gigs around town. Through referrals by his mentor, Johnny Smith, and fellow jazz guitarist Mundell Lowe, Salvador played in the Radio City Music Hall Orchestra and became a staff musician with Columbia Records accompanying Ella Fitzgerald, Sarah Vaughan, Tony Bennett, and many other well-known vocalists.

Bandleader Stan Kenton hired Salvador in 1952 to tour the country and record as a featured soloist with the Stan Kenton Orchestra. He is recognized most famously for "Frivolous Sal" and his fiery performance in the progressive composition "Invention for Guitar and Trumpet" with Maynard Ferguson (which was used in the movie *Blackboard Jungle*). Recording as a leader followed, with his first album titled *Sal Salvador Quintet*, for Blue Note in 1953. The following year he recorded *Kenton Presents Sal Salvador* with Morello and pianist/vibist Eddie Costa. He enjoyed the diversity of performing with both small groups and big bands.

In 1958 he appeared in the film *Jazz on a Summer's Day* playing with saxophonist Sonny Stitt at the Newport Jazz Festival. The same year, Salvador introduced his own big band on the Decca release *Colors in Sound* (artists included Doc Severinsen and Maynard Ferguson). The Colors in Sound Orchestra toured and recorded until the mid-1960s to critical praise. His was the first band ever to use the mellophonium. Extensive touring as an accompanist for such entertainers as Martin and Lewis, Robert Goulet and Johnny Mathis, as well as a 36-state tour with his own quartet completed the '60s.

His unquenchable thirst for musical knowledge enabled him to master the guitar to the extent that he was commissioned to develop his own method of teaching the instrument. This resulted in over 20 best-selling instruction books. Many are standard texts for guitar students. Originally released in 1962, *The Complete Chord Book* and this book, *Sal Salvador's Single String Studies*, have become classics used by beginners and professionals alike. The books were part of his curriculum at both The University of Bridgeport and Western Connecticut State University where he taught, ran the jazz guitar ensembles and was head of the guitar departments.

Sal recorded a number of albums in the '70s and '80s with his small groups, and guitar duos that included many highly regarded artists. Most have been re-released on CD, including two in 2015 by Mosaic Records as part of their *Complete Bee Hive Sessions* box set. This contains the album *Juicy Lucy*, again featuring lifelong friend Joe Morello on drums.

Salvador formed the band Crystal Image in 1992. Their debut album was his 19th release. Exploring again, this new group offered a fresh sound with complex arrangements, asymmetrical phrasing and the unique harmonies of scat vocal parts layered with two guitars. The second guitarist was longtime collaborator Mike Giordano. Crystal Image received great critical acclaim for their recordings and concerts.

Sal was recognized numerous times by the *Playboy* jazz poll and *Guitar Player* magazine as an outstanding jazz artist and his compositions have received many awards. He endorsed the Sal Salvador signature model Gretsch guitar. Starting in the 1970s, he joined forces with luthier Carl Barney to design a Sal Salvador handcrafted, artist model which became Sal's preferred guitar. The model was also made available as part of Carl's fine custom guitar line. Avenues where he shared his knowledge included columns in *Guitar Player*, Hot Licks instructional videos and as a contributing consultant for *Just Jazz Guitar*. He taught jazz clinics at many prominent universities and the Stan Kenton jazz camps, performed JVC Jazz Festival tribute shows with other luminaries, and his own concerts throughout his career.

From the '50s through the '90s he continuously taught privately in Connecticut and New York City. Many of Sal's students have gone on to major success in their own right.

He always reminded his students of the importance of practicing with the goal of developing their own, individual style of playing. "Don't make practice a laborious thing. The feeling of accomplishment that comes from practicing something and then being able to play it well is a reward in itself. A lot of it is in your outlook. Music is a beautiful thing when played properly and practicing to achieve this can be fun."

CONTENTS

FOREWORDS

Sal Salvador was my third and final guitar teacher. By the time I'd met him in 1963, I was the epitome of the young hot rock guitarist with lots of "chops", aspirations ...and opinions. My first lesson, which was a combination of introduction / audition / consultation, left me in absolute awe. It was clear that there was so much that I could learn from this outgoing, humorous, generous and brilliant musician, that I was in for a very important life experience. And you know, it wasn't always easy. Sal's standards are extremely high, and we had no choice but to meet these standards head-on, I will always be grateful for this.

Here is a method book that will both challenge and delight the user – for a lifetime. I say this from personal experience; when I pull out my copy (generally for my late-night wood-shedding), I realise that it's been in my hands – and on my music stands for over half a century now! I've kept my original copy in good shape for a reason: it keeps me in good shape.

There is a lot to be said for combinations of exercises that develop and retain muscle memory and at the same time consistently remind the player that they are *never* lost on the fretboard. Sal's work in formulating this book accomplishes exactly that. Having just described some of the advantages to the fretting hand, I can assure you that the picking hand is given as many challenges, hence a sense of "completeness" to Sal's methodology.

As an interesting aside, world-renowned jazz guitarists John Tropea and Louis Volpe (or "King Louie" as many of us called him) were students of Sal's at the same time – what a great place to first meet! I recall with great warmth, the mood in the waiting room of Sal's teaching studio on West 46th Street. It was always warm, friendly and full of jazz jokes. Halcyon times.

Now turn to the first page of exercises and begin slowly. What we are aiming for here is accuracy. The more *consistently* you work at these, you'll find that your speed – and confidence will increase commensurately. Enjoy the ride.

Elliott Randall
Steely Dan, Randall's Island, Music Consultant for NBC *Saturday Night Live* (1975-81) and others

Throughout our lives, no matter what road we choose, or what vocation we're born into, we never forget the great teachers we have had.

When I met Sal Salvador, and he took me on as one of his students, I was 16 years old and I'd already been playing for 7 years, but I wanted to be a really great guitar player.

With my first teacher, Gene Dell, I went through the complete Mel Bay Course, one book after another. I had never studied out of 9 books at a time before Sal. Is he kidding? *George Van Eps Guitar Techniques*, *Phil Krauss' Mallet Methods*, *Johnny Smith Interpretations*, *Sal Salvador's Complete Chord Book*, a few others I need to remember, and *Sal Salvador's Single String Studies*.

I never thought I'd get through studying that way, but by the time we parted company, I wasn't just a guitar player anymore. I had actually become a guitarist. It took me a while to realize it. Perhaps if I hadn't been so worried that my guitar would get stolen every week on the subway back to Queens after my lesson, I would have known then just how much confidence he had instilled in me, and also how much ability he brought out of me.

We never forget the great teachers we have had. And I certainly will never forget to say, "Thank you again Sal."

Waddy Wachtel
Warren Zevon, James Taylor, Linda Ronstadt, Stevie Nicks, Keith Richards and others

MUSIC NOTATION USED IN THIS BOOK

In addition to standard music notation, tablature (or *tab*) has been added to accompany the examples in this book. Tablature is a graphical system designed for the guitar, indicating the string and fret where each note is played. Each line of the tab staff represents a string on the guitar; the lowest line of the staff corresponds to the 6th (lowest-pitched) string on the guitar, and the highest line of the staff corresponds to the 1st (highest-pitched) string on the guitar.

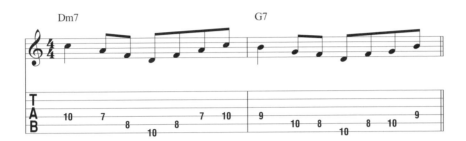

In addition to tab, many of the examples in this book include fret-hand fingering to clarify which fingers to use while fretting the notes. When necessary, finger numbers will be added between the notation and tab staff: 1 = index finger, 2 = middle finger, 3 = ring finger, 4 = pinky finger.

Examples will also include position indications to further clarify hand positions on the fretboard. Roman numerals are used to indicate the position. For example, II will be used to indicate second position, meaning that the first finger of your fret hand should be placed at the second fret. Some examples also include circled numbers above the notation to indicate the strings on the guitar.

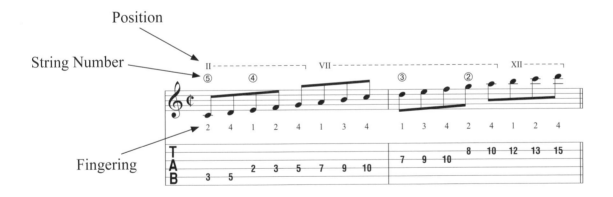

Picking symbols are used to indicate downstrokes (⊓) or upstrokes (∨) with the pick.

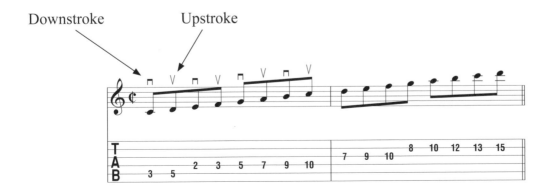

MAJOR SCALES AND VARIATIONS

ONE OCTAVE MAJOR SCALES AND EXERCISES

Practice all exercises slowly. Accuracy is far more important than speed. Once you have gained accuracy, the speed will come automatically. When crossing strings with the same finger, roll instead of lifting and refretting. In this manner, the legato sound is kept constant. Watch the picking carefully. All scales and variations in the section are to be practiced chromatically. Fingering for each note of the variations is the same as in the basic scale.

Ex. 1

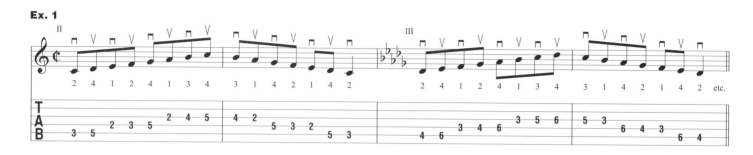

Ex. 2

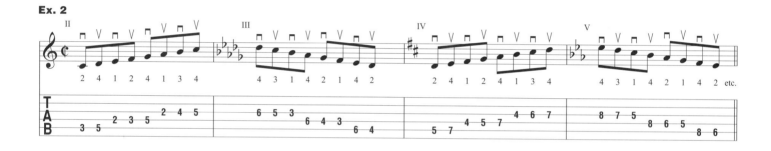

Ex. 3

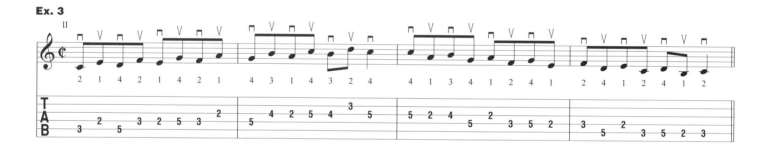

Ex. 4

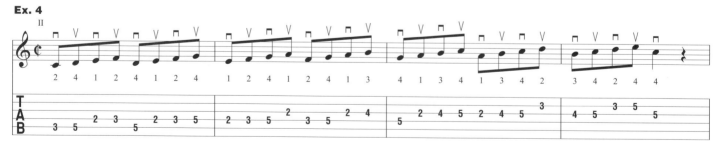

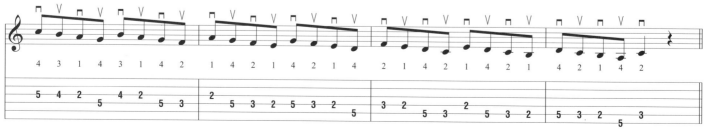

Ex. 5

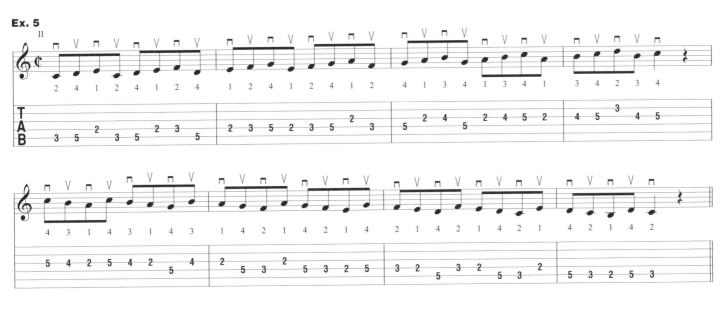

Ex. 6

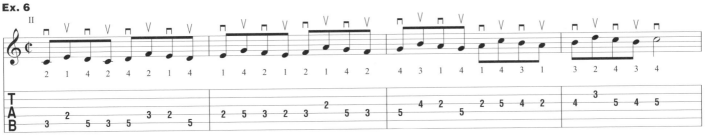

Use the same fingering as the previous exercises.

Ex. 7

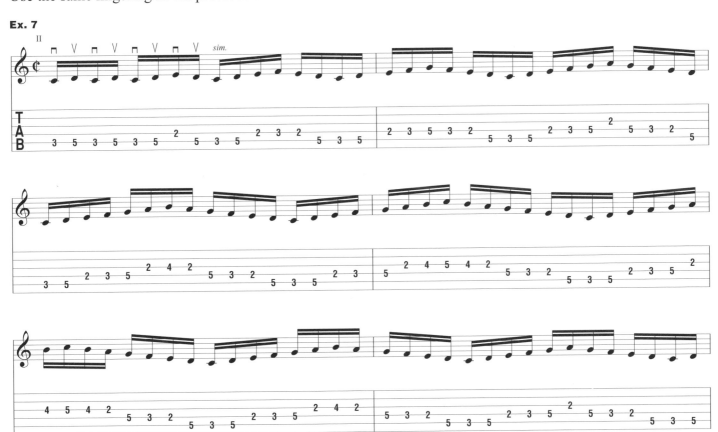

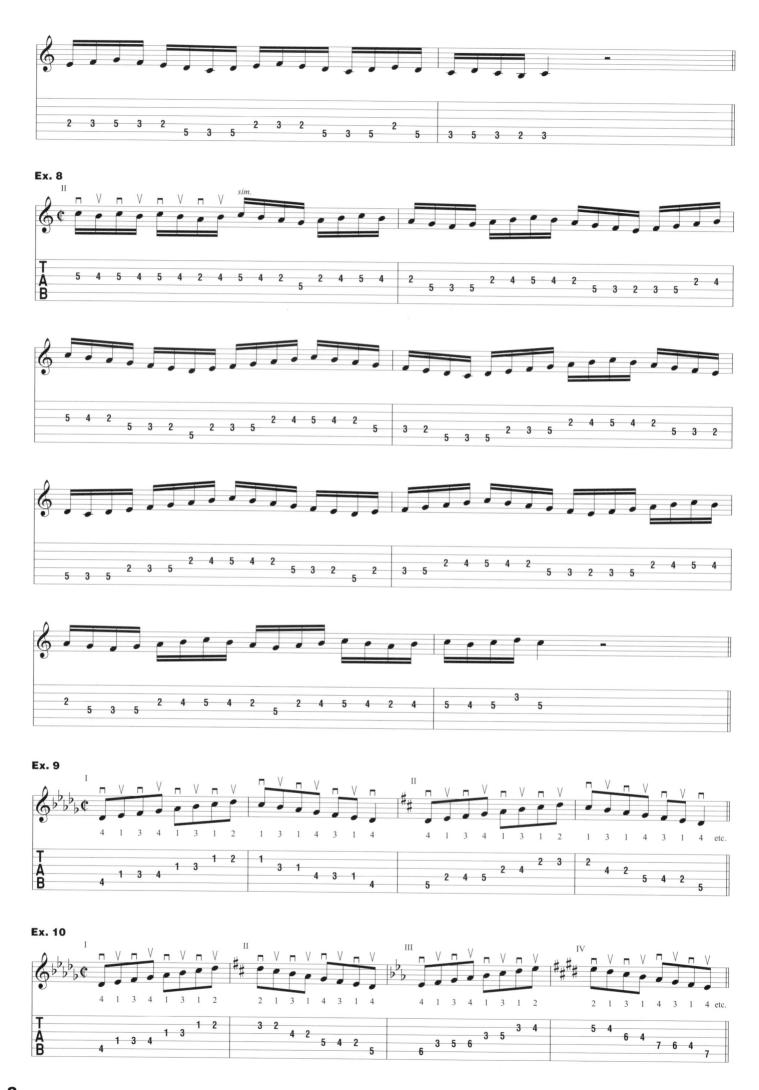

Ex. 8

Ex. 9

Ex. 10

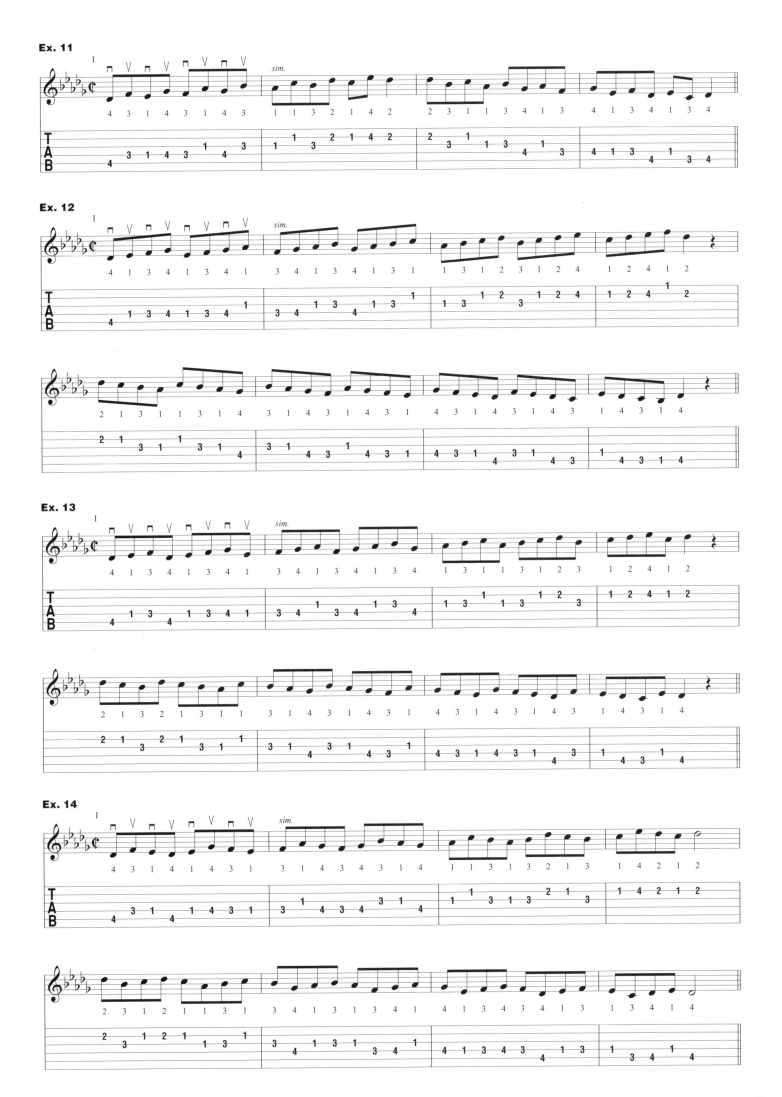

Use the same fingering as the previous exercises.

Ex. 15

Ex. 16

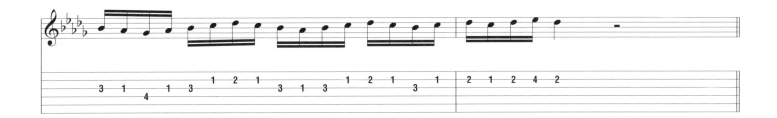

TWO OCTAVE MAJOR SCALES AND EXERCISES

The same rules apply here as in the one octave scales.

Ex. 17

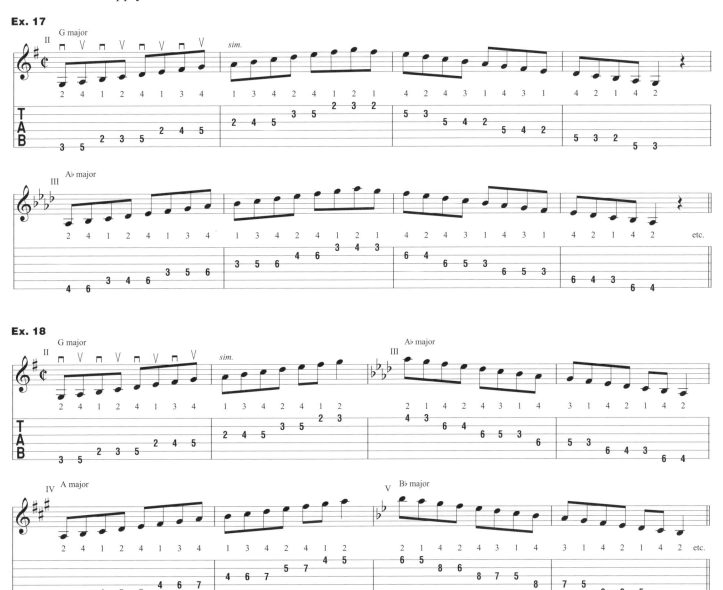

Ex. 18

Ex. 19

Practice chromatically.

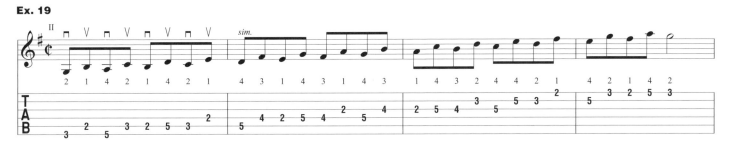

Use the same fingering as the previous exercises.

Ex. 20

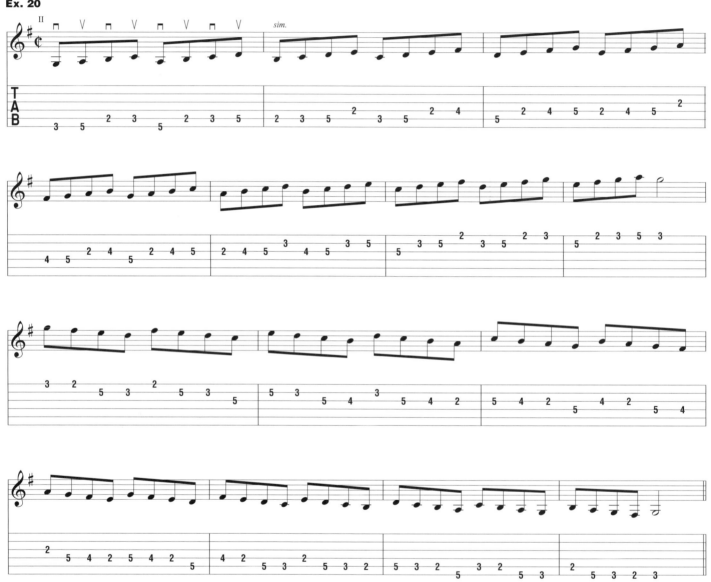

Use the same fingering; practice chromatically.

Ex. 21

Use the same fingering; practice chromatically.

Ex. 22

Perform these exercises up and down throughout. Play as marked, then reverse.

Ex. 23

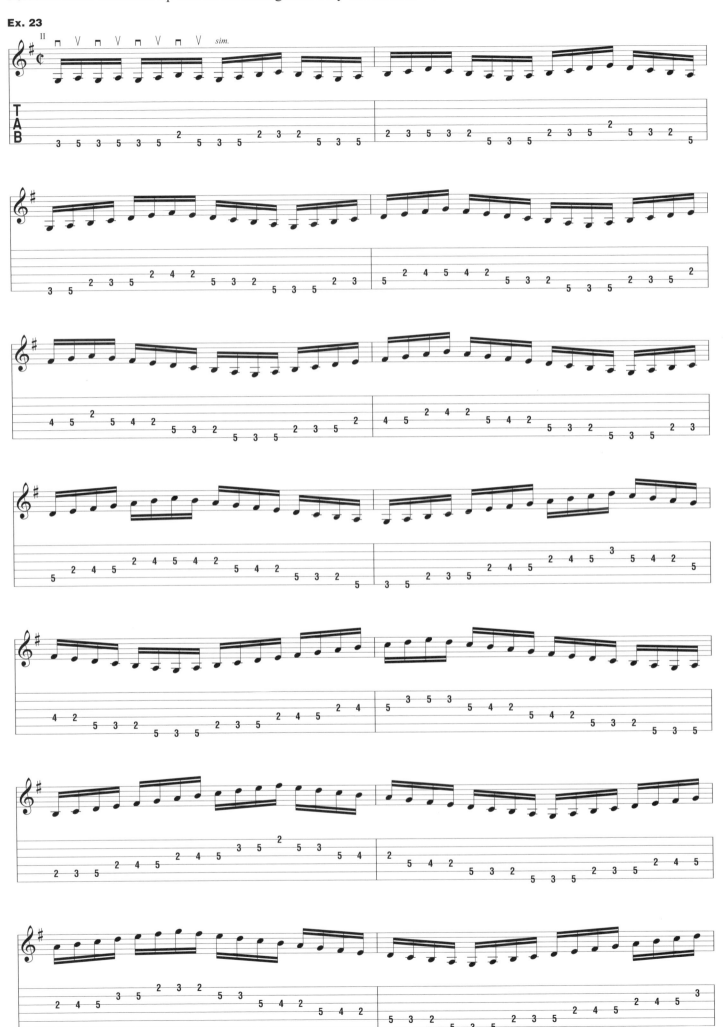

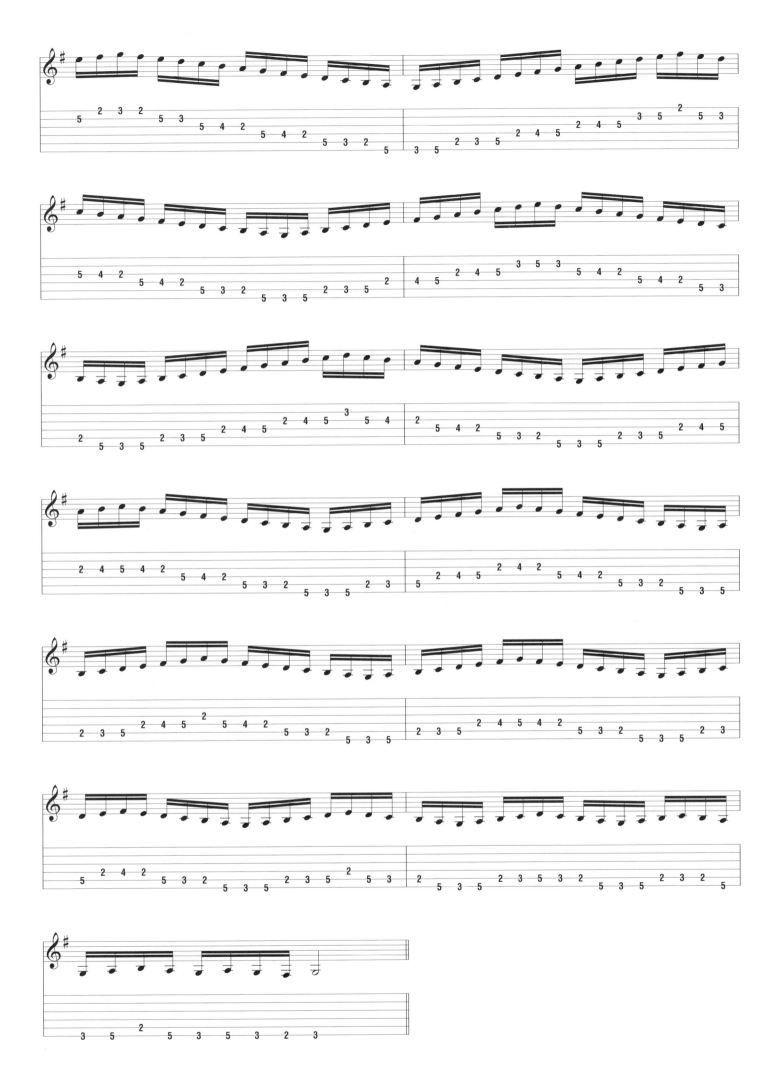

Ex. 24

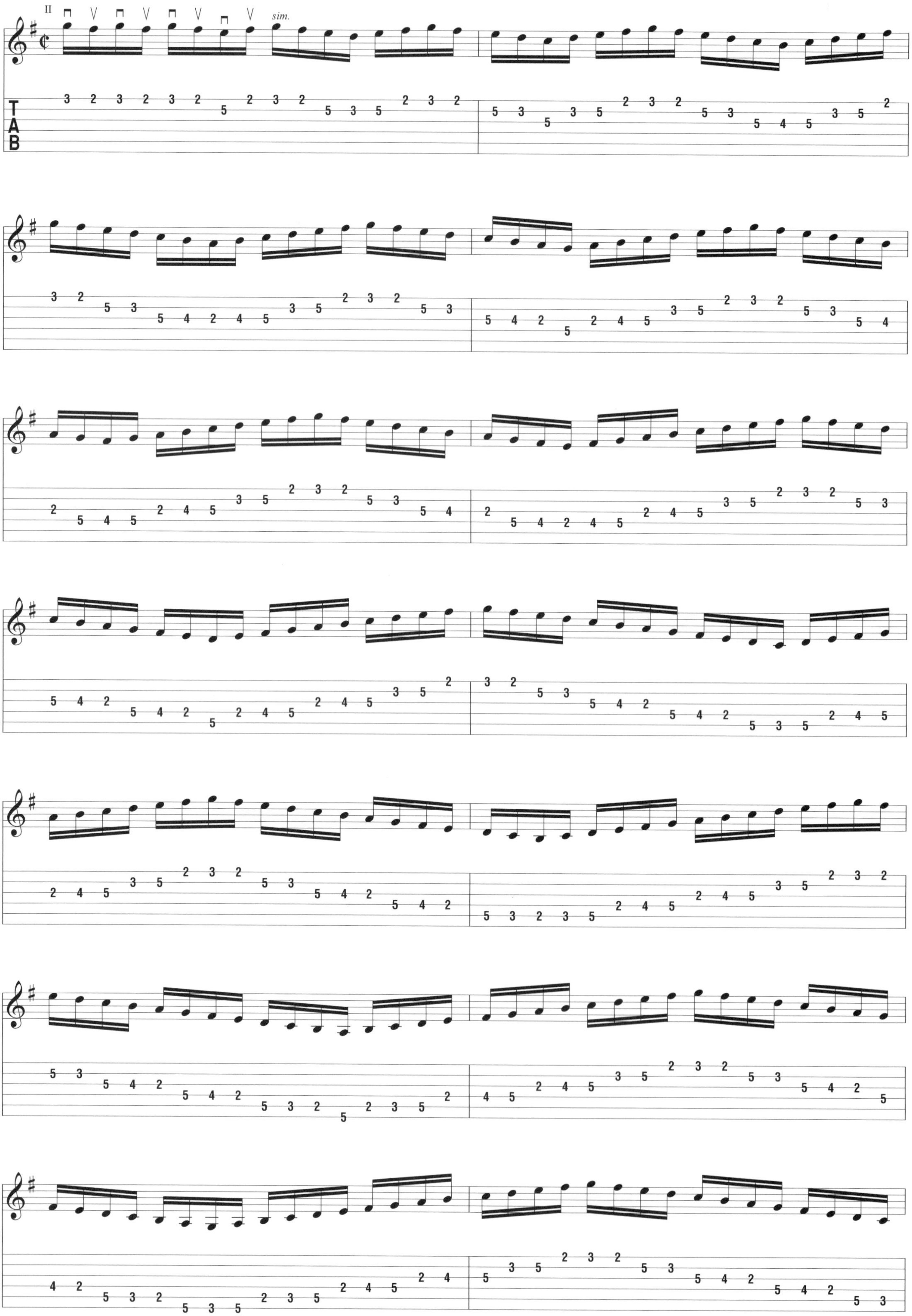

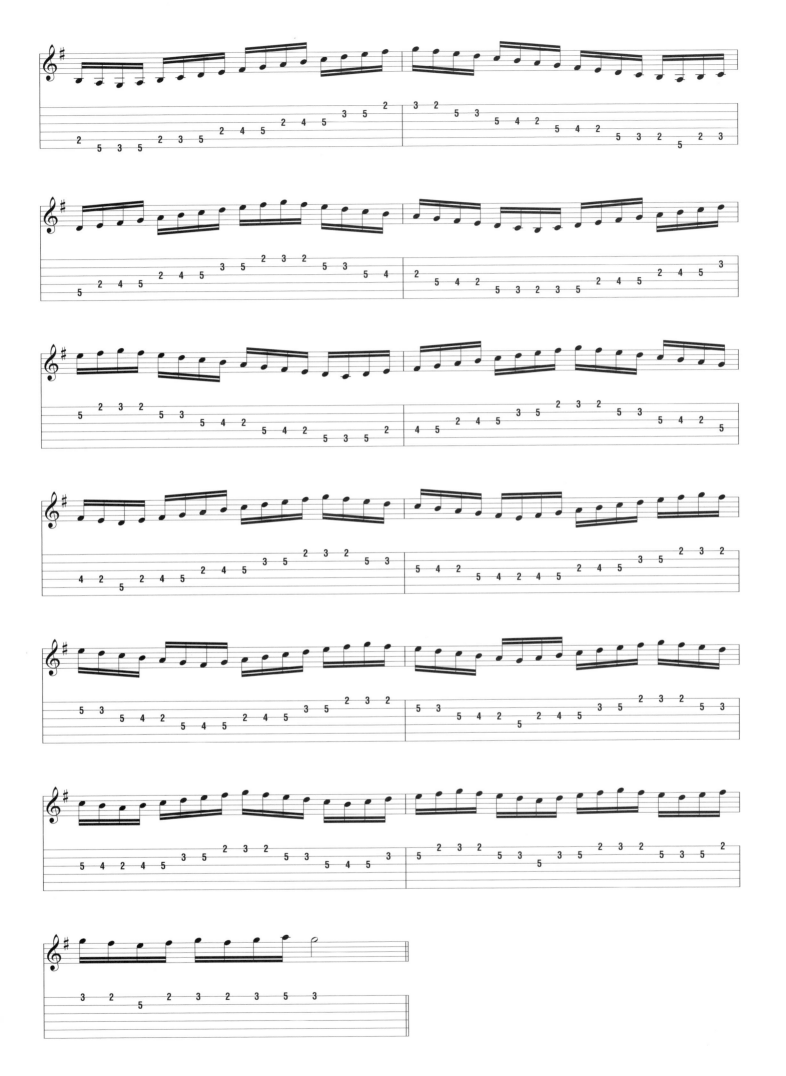

Ex. 25

Ex. 26

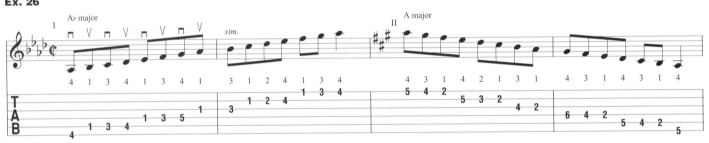

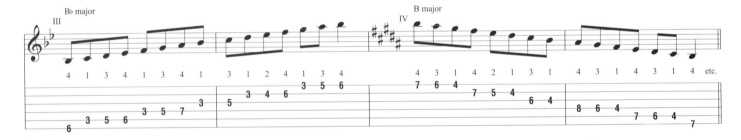

Practice chromatically.

Ex. 27

Use the same fingering; practice chromatically.

Ex. 28

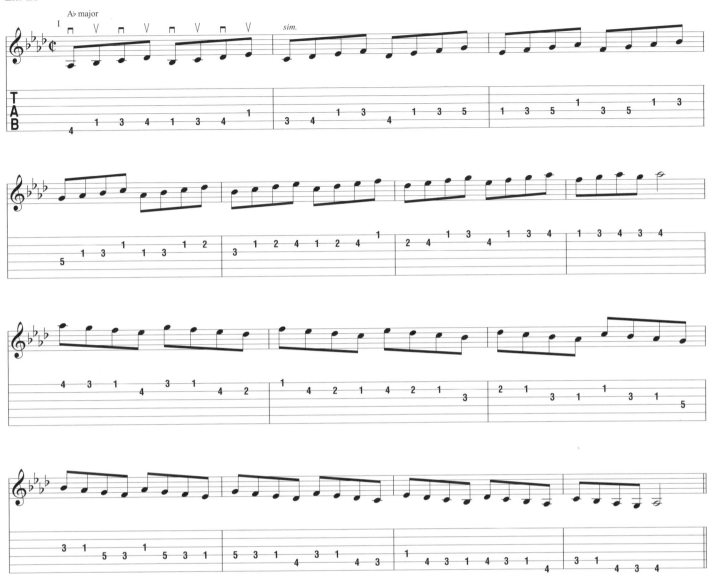

Use the same fingering; practice chromatically.

Ex. 29

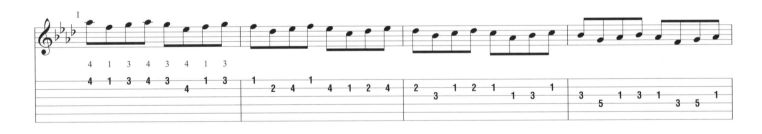

Use the same fingering; practice chromatically.

Ex. 30

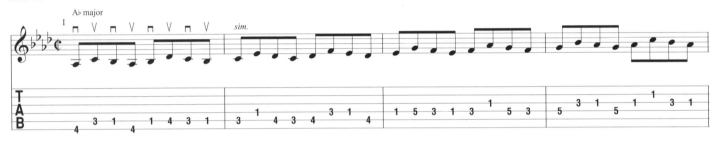

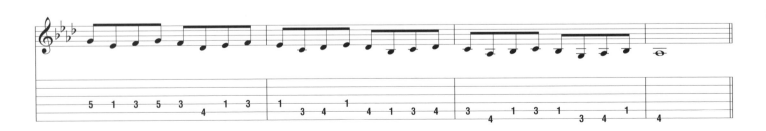

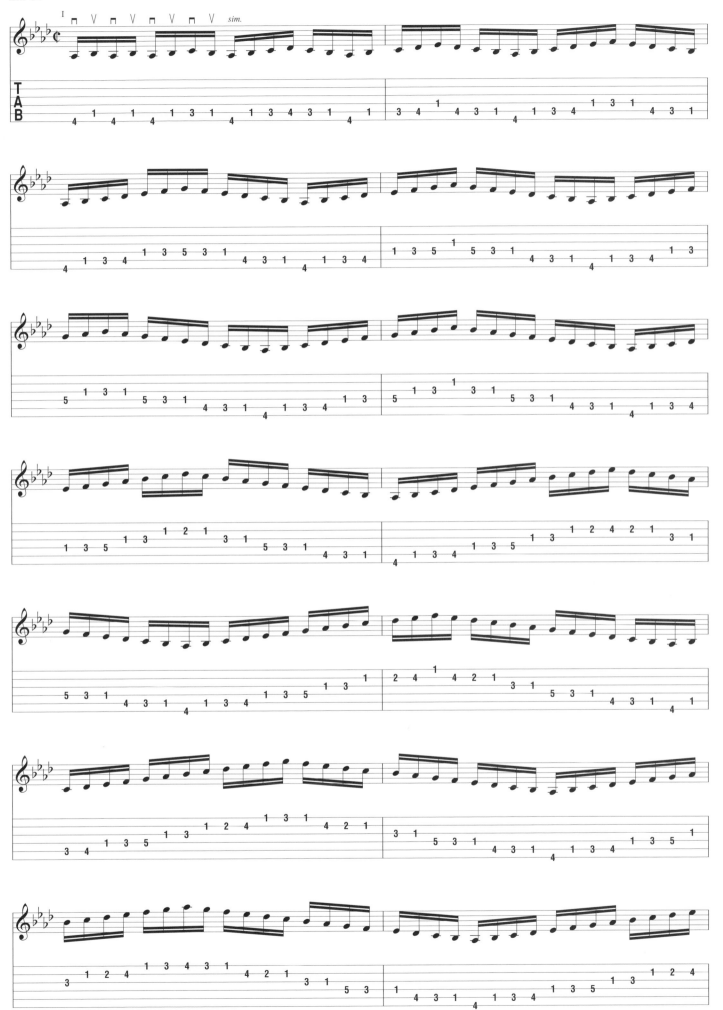

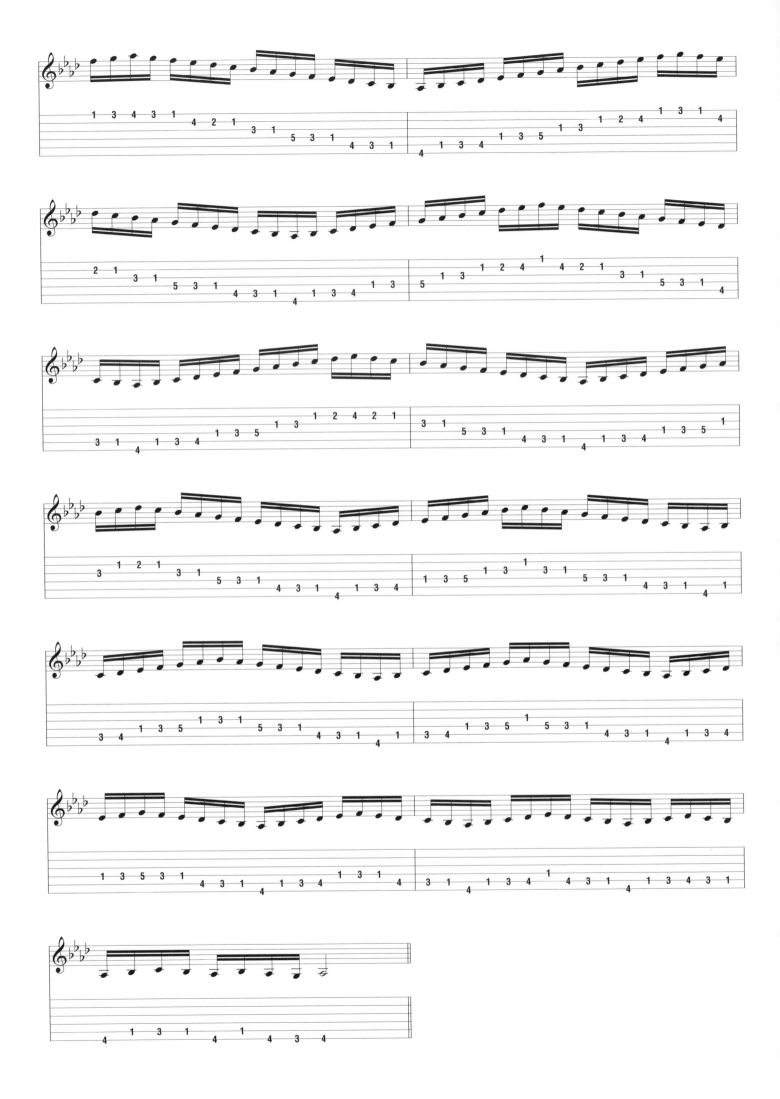

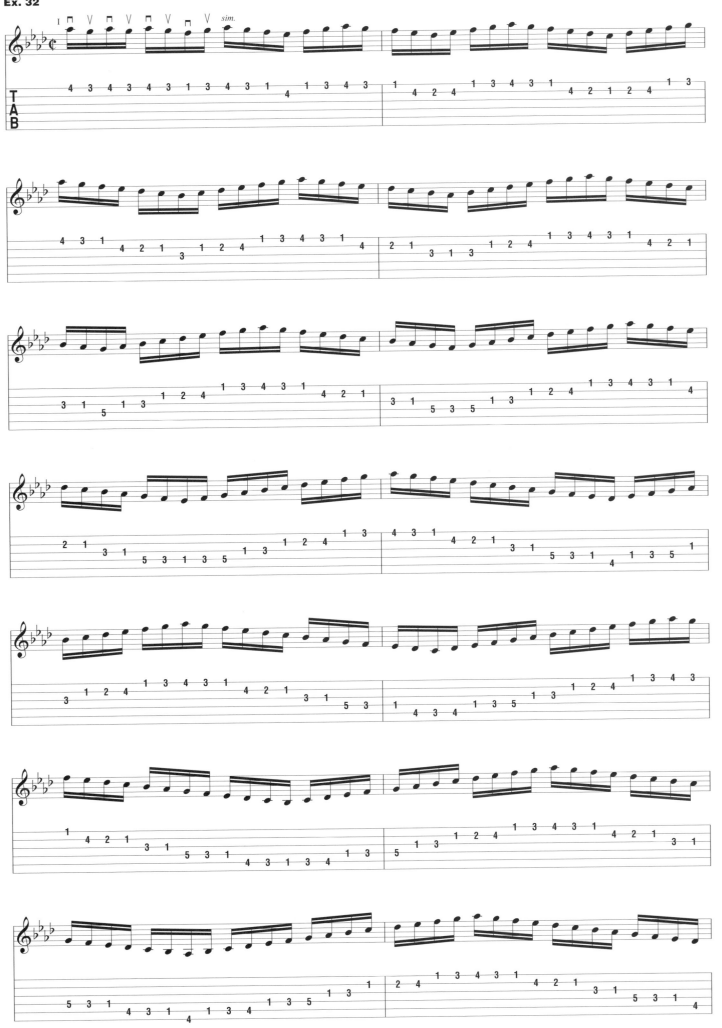

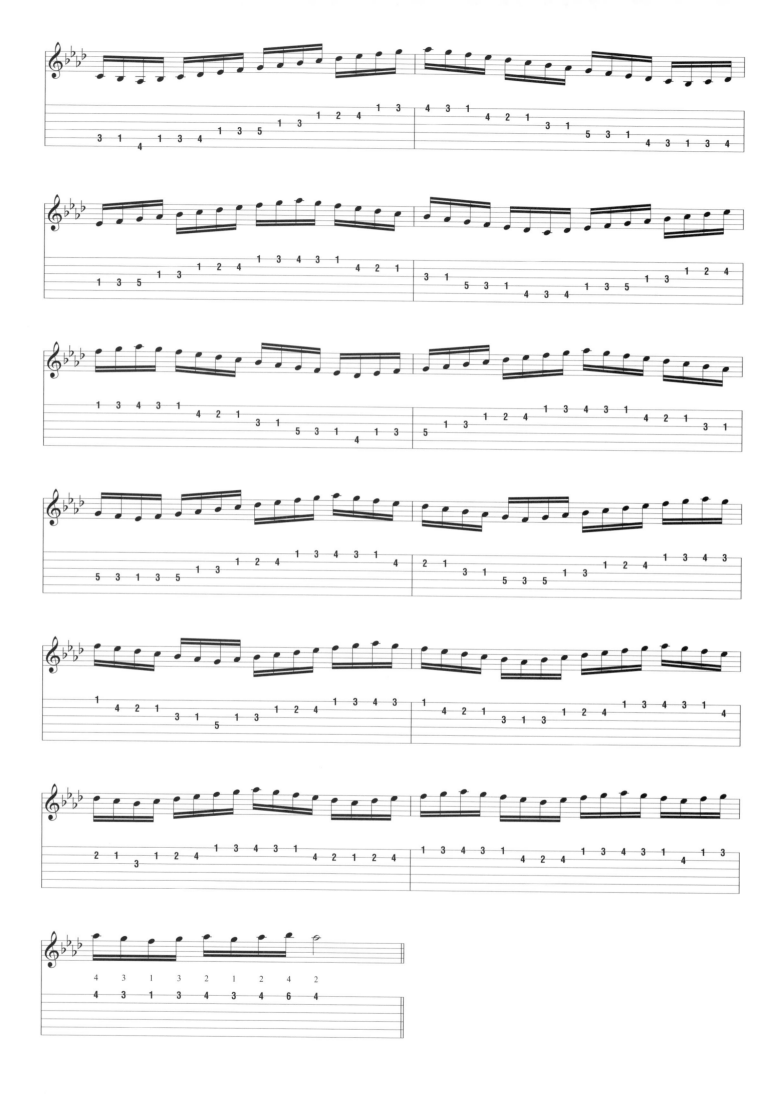

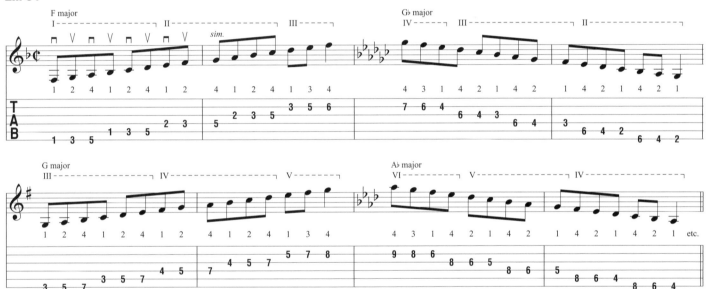

Practice chromatically.

Use the same fingering; practice chromatically.

Ex. 36

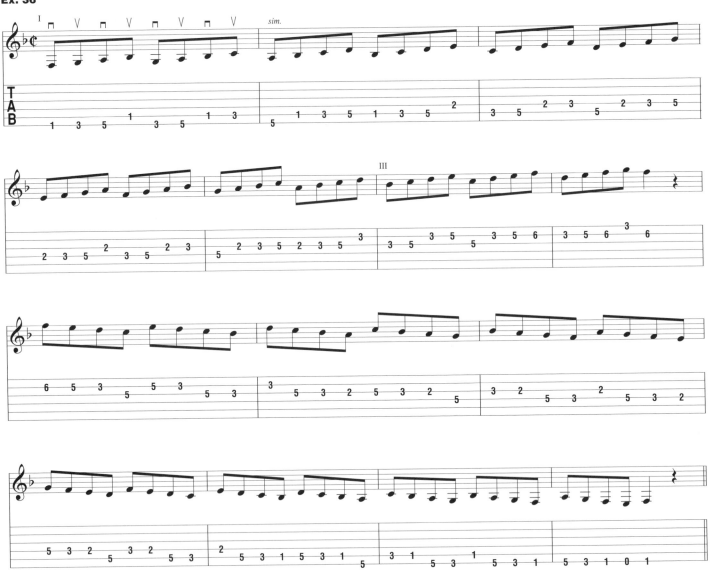

Use the same fingering; practice chromatically.

Ex. 37

Use the same fingering; practice chromatically.

Ex. 38

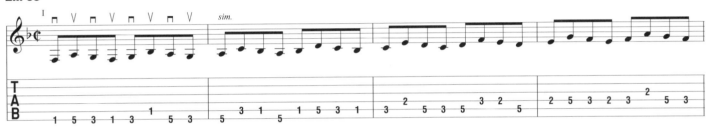

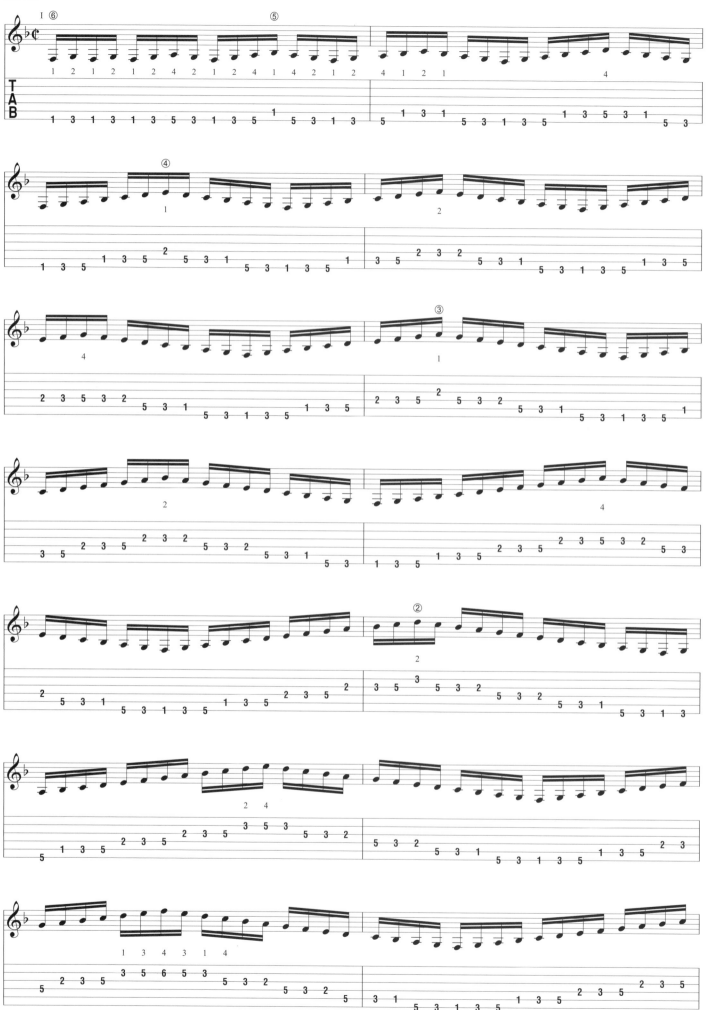

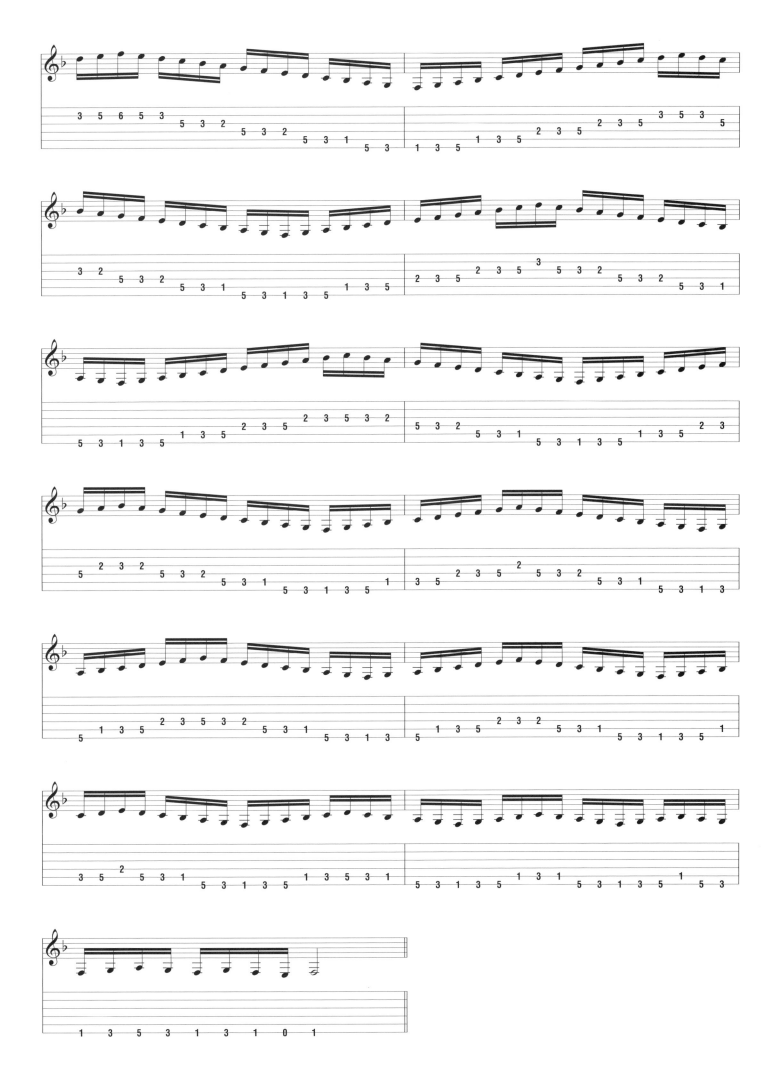

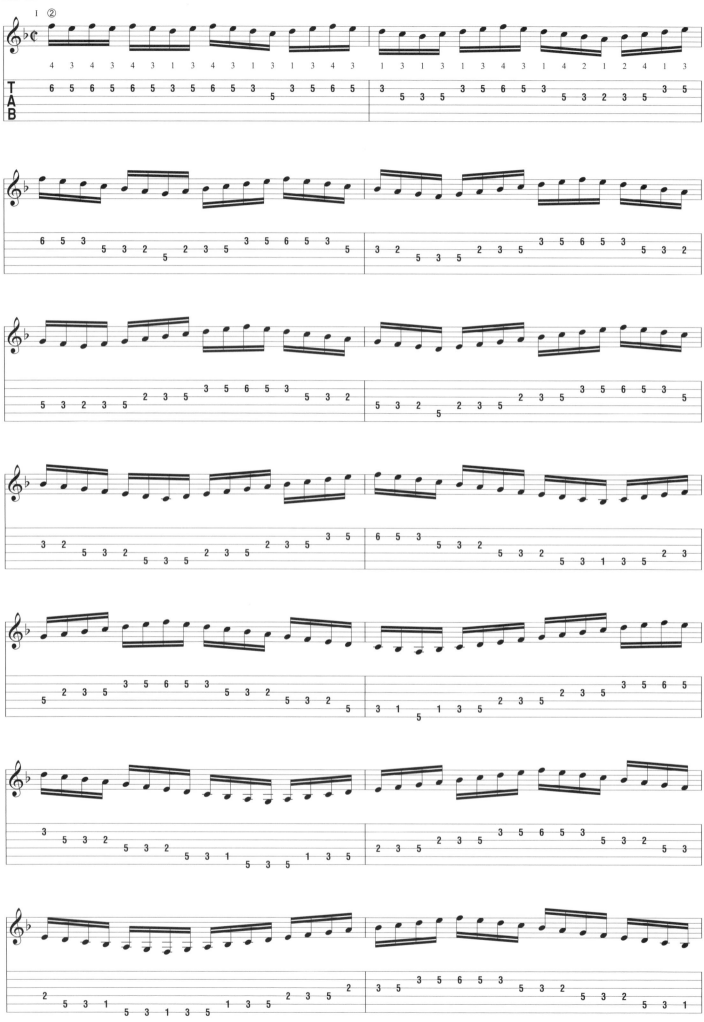

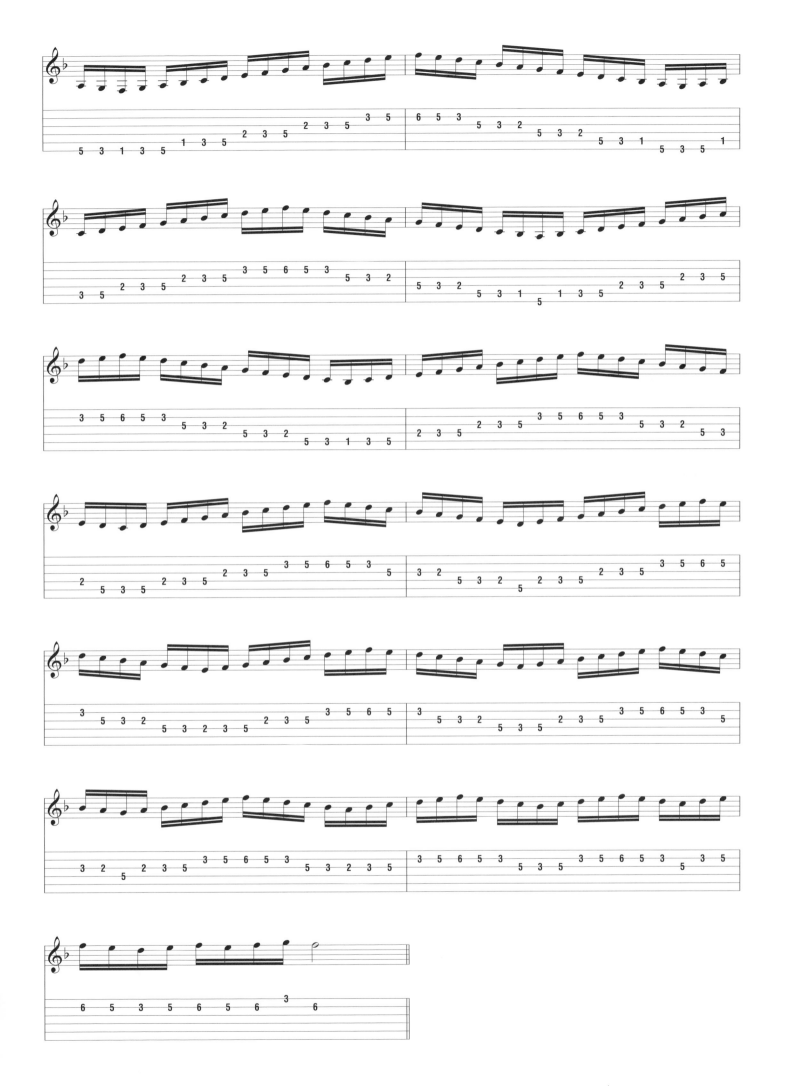

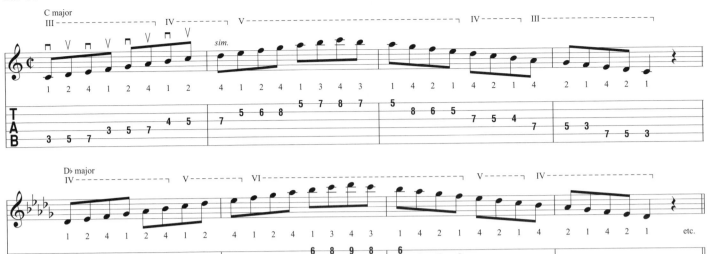

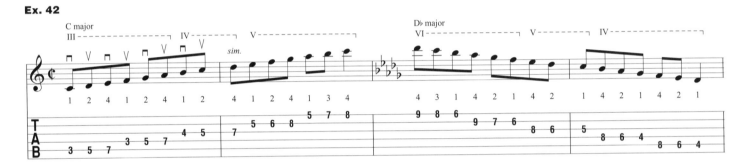

Ex. 42

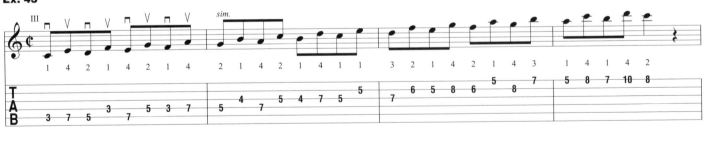

Practice chromatically.

Ex. 43

Use the same fingering; practice chromatically.

Ex. 44

Use the same fingering; practice chromatically.

Ex. 45

Use the same fingering; practice chromatically.

Ex. 46

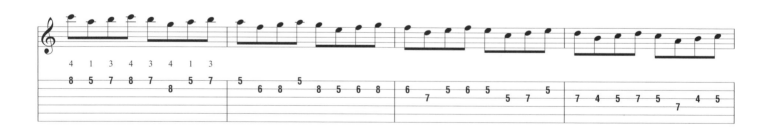

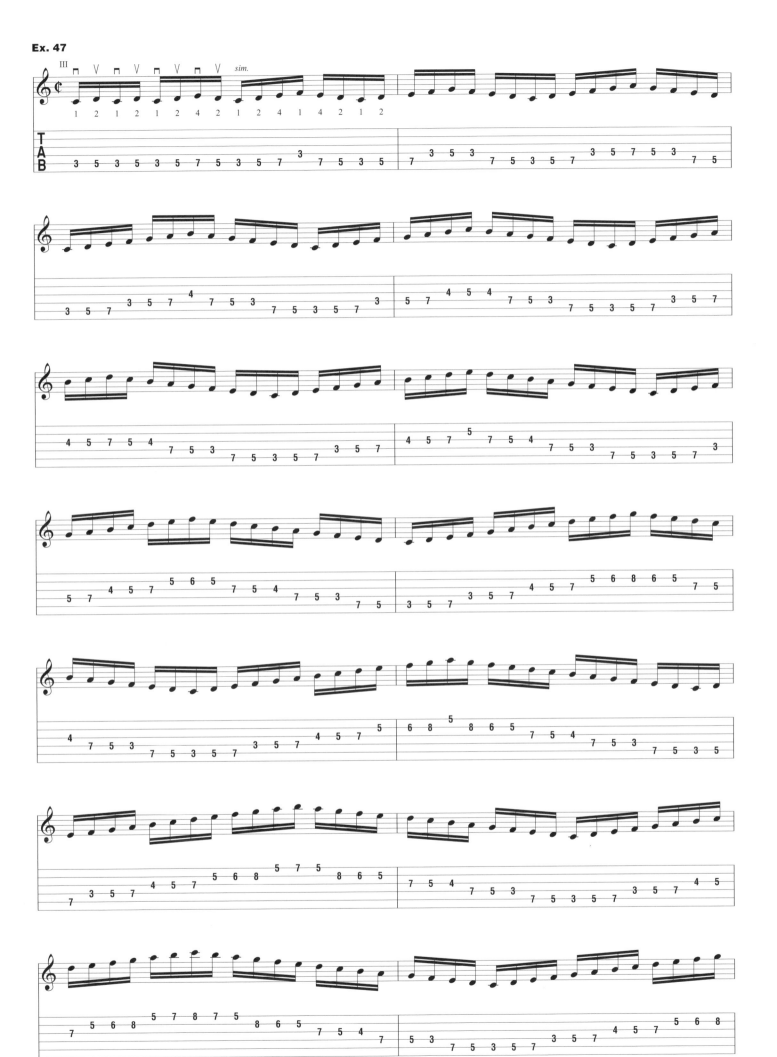

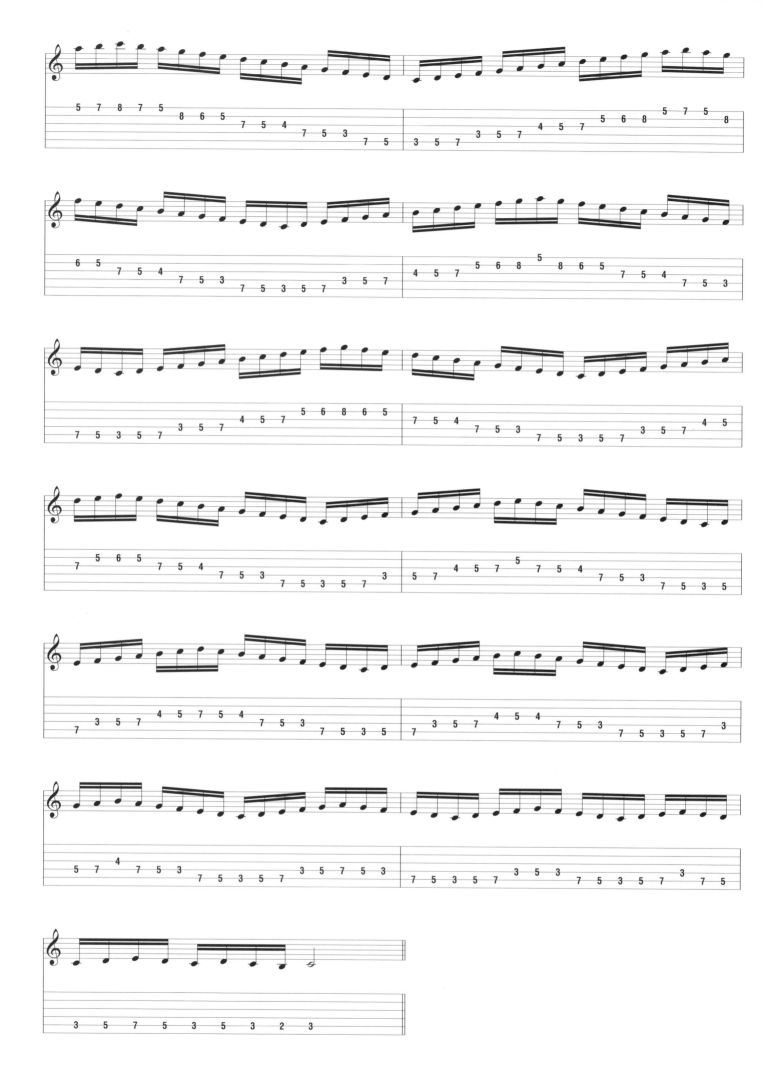

VARIATIONS ON THE MAJOR SCALE

Ex. 48

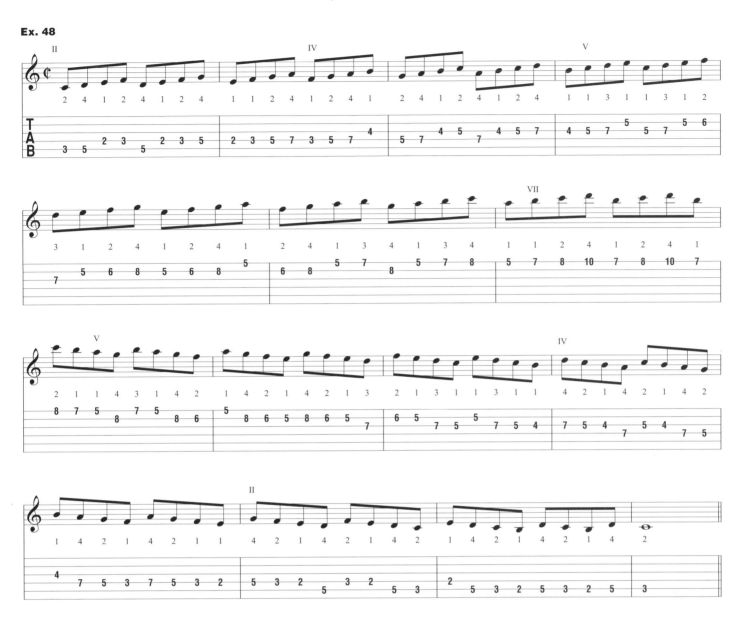

DIFFERENT FINGERINGS

Ex. 49

Ex. 50

VARIATIONS

Ex. 51

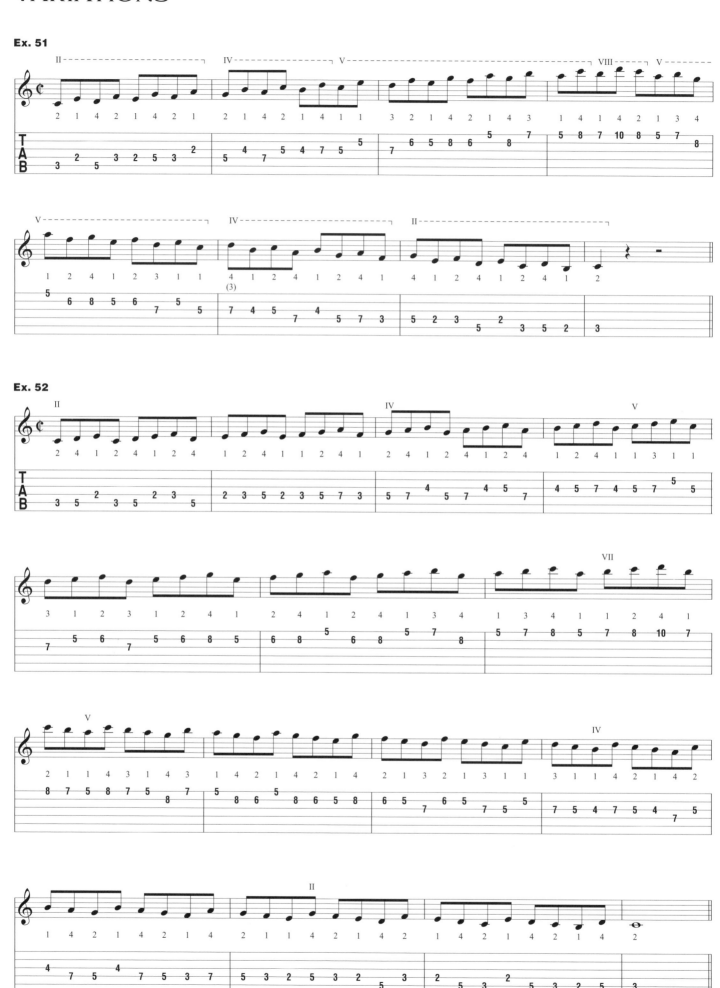

Ex. 52

THREE SCALES TO BE PRACTICED CHROMATICALLY

Watch carefully for slight differences in the fingering of the scales.

Ex. 53

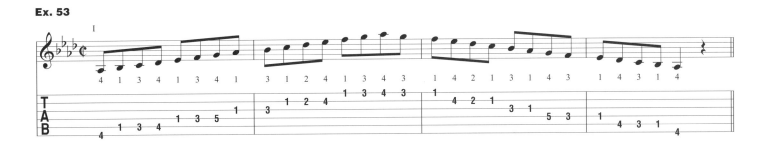

Ex. 54

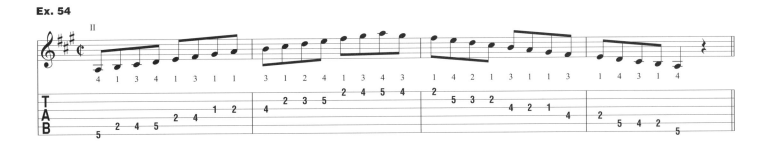

Ex. 55

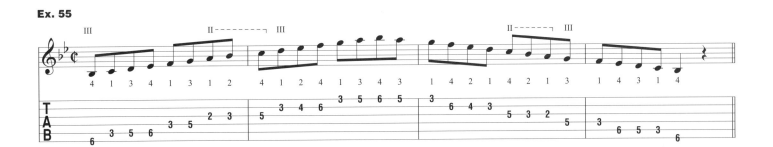

MAJOR SCALES IN LONG FORM (SKIPPING POSITIONS)

The scales in the following section should be practiced very slowly and carefully at first so there won't be any slurring or other noises when changing positions. This is a very good warm-up set of exercises for every day, no matter how long you've been playing. Remember that accuracy is the most important thing at first. The speed will come automatically.

All of the scales have been presented in eighth-note rhythm (two notes per beat). After you have memorized all of the scales, you may play them more rapidly. First try them in a 16th-note rhythm (four notes per beat), then in a fast, 16th-note triplet rhythm (six notes per beat).

Play these scales only with alternate picking, which should not change at any time whether crossing strings or not. A good rule to remember is to use downstrokes on the "down" of a beat and upstrokes on the "up" of a beat. This applies everywhere except for a few special instances. For reading convenience, each example contains Roman numerals and dashed lines above the notation to clarify the positions changes. Refer to these indications in addition to the tab and finger numbering to properly switch positions when ascending and descending the scales.

Ex. 56

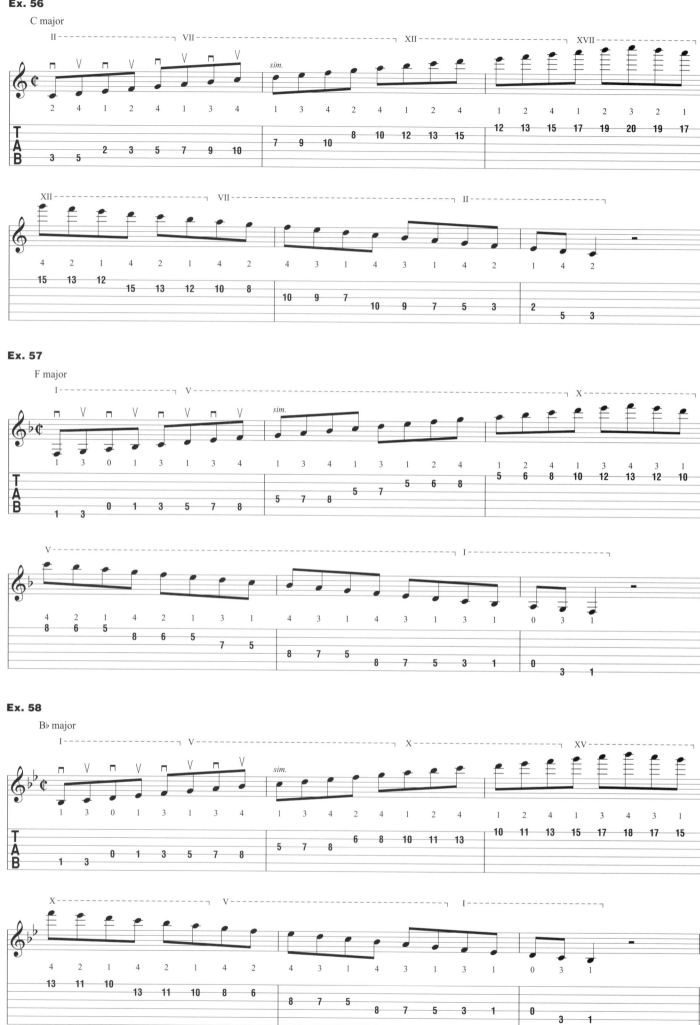

Ex. 59

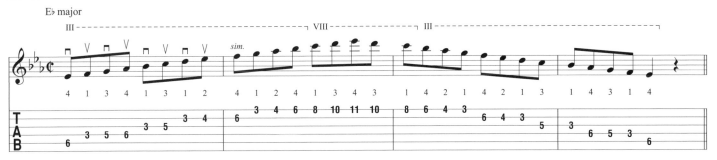

Ex. 60

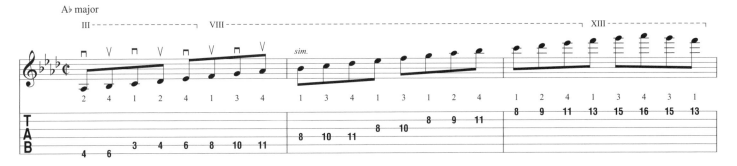

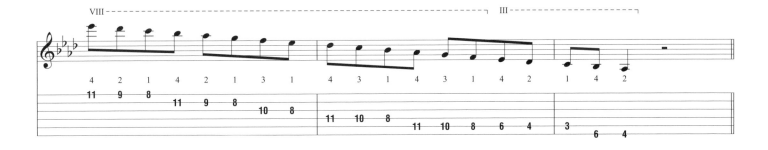

Ex. 61

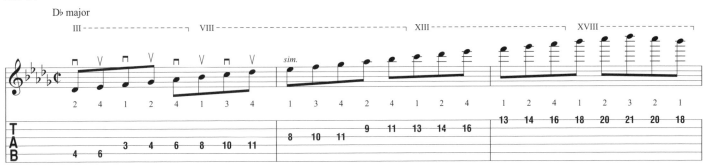

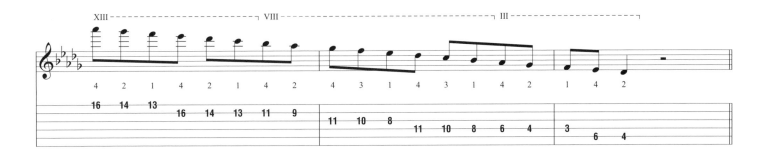

Ex. 62

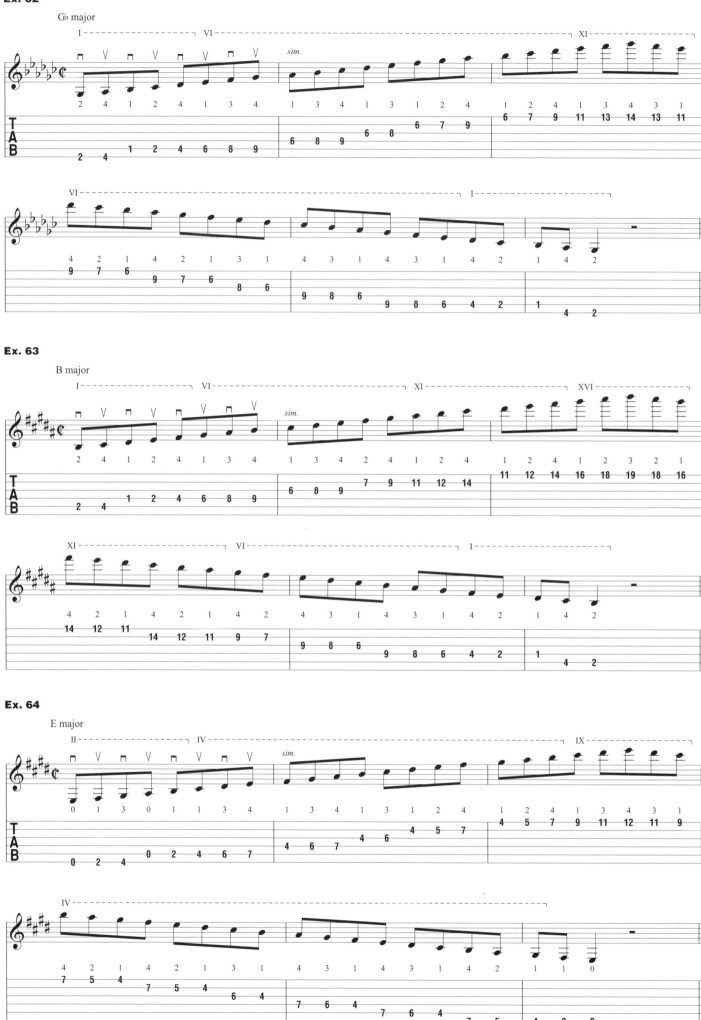

Ex. 63

Ex. 64

Ex. 65

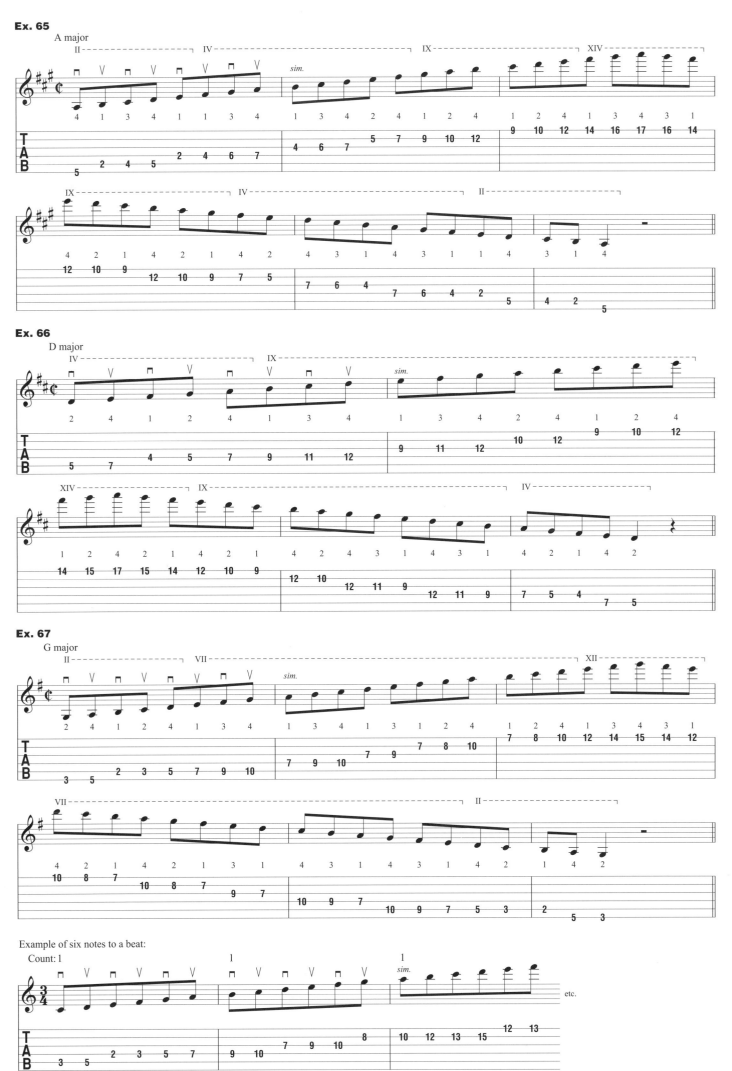

CHROMATIC SCALES

Ex. 68

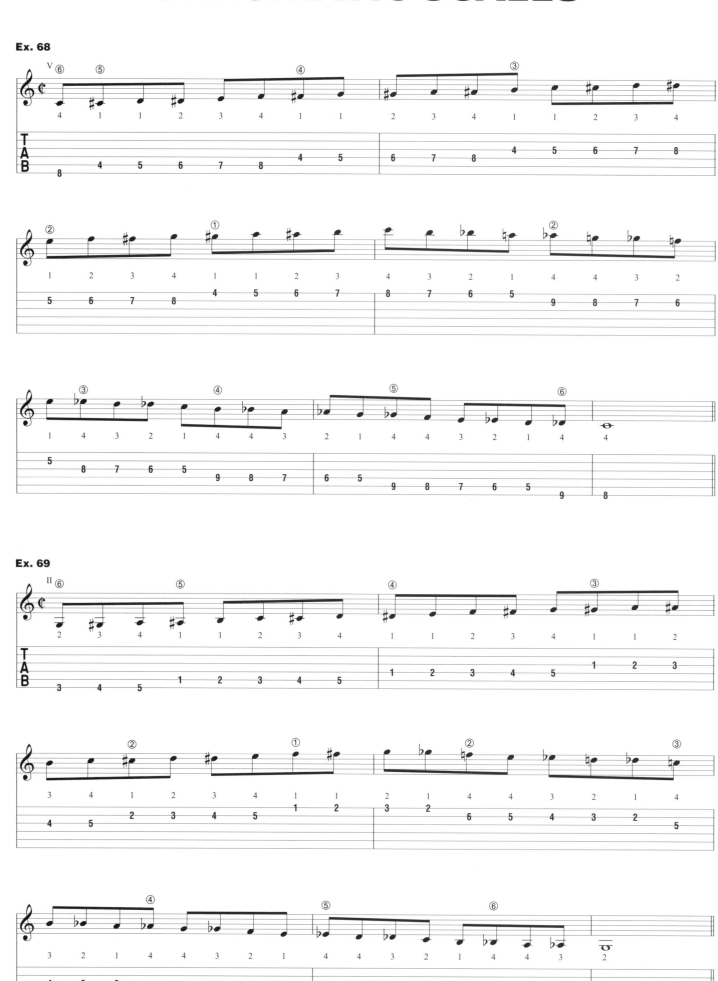

Ex. 69

Ex. 70

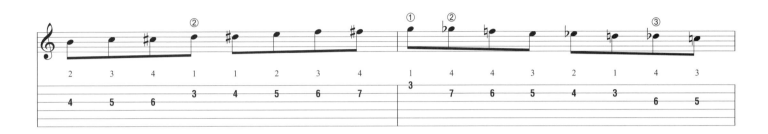

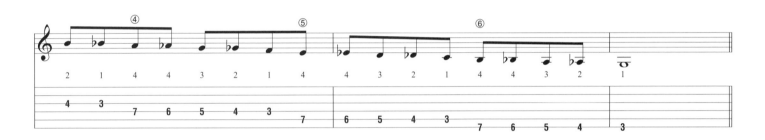

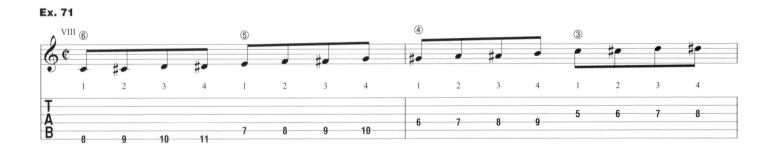

Ex. 71

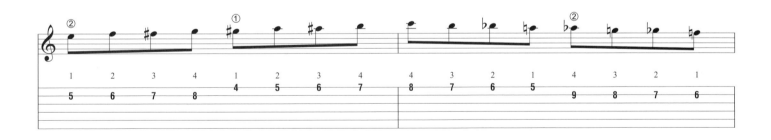

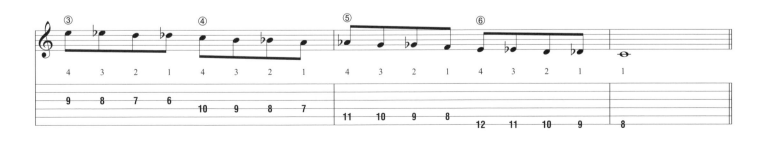

TECHNICAL EXERCISES

TREMOLO EXERCISES

The importance of tremolo exercises cannot be overemphasized. They are very helpful for the picking hand, which is one of the major components of guitar playing. In the following exercises, use fast, consistent alternate picking. The tremolo has been rhythmically indicated here using 32nd notes. The three examples use various fret-hand fingerings of the major scale.

Ex. 72

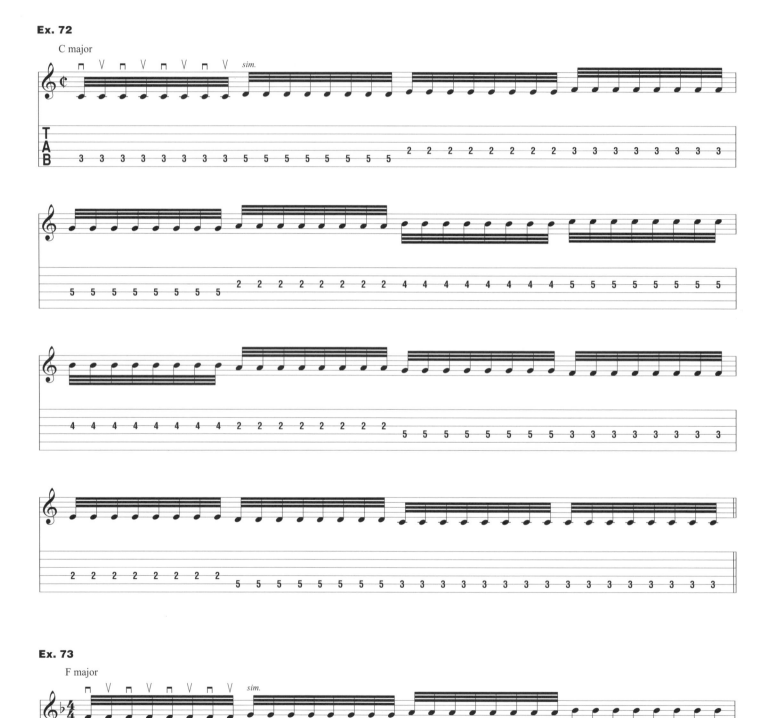

Ex. 73

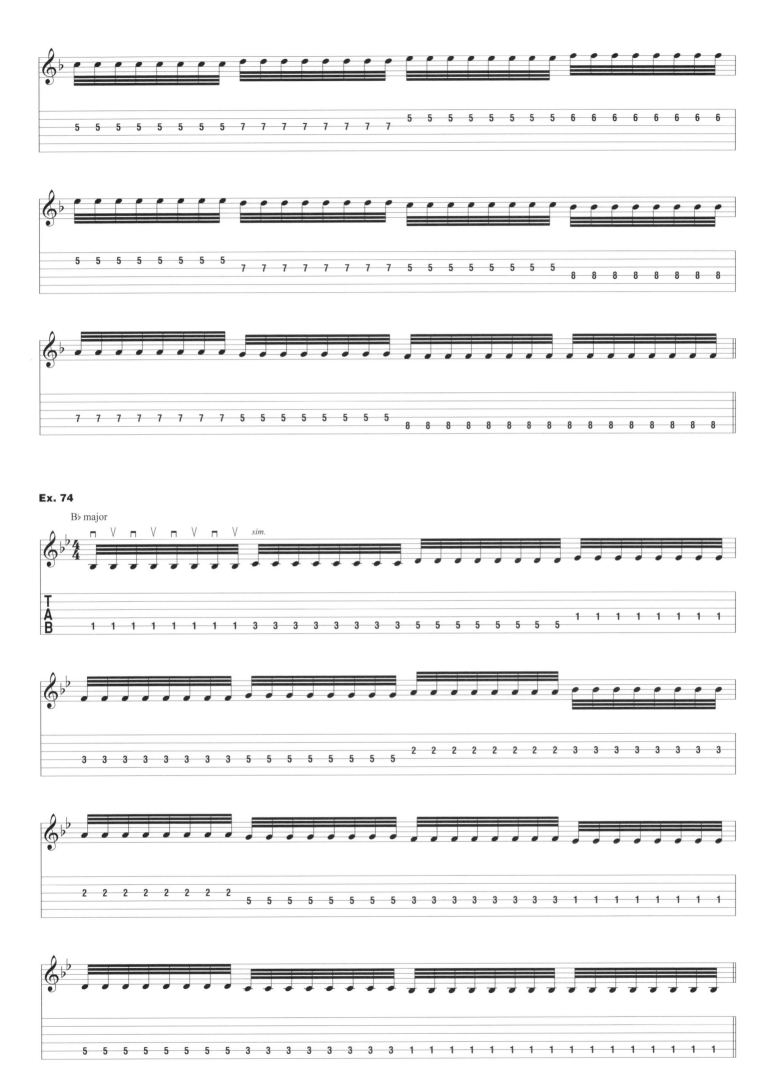

Ex. 74

B♭ major

Tremolo is often notated using a short-hand system. The number of lines above the whole note shown below indicate the speed of the tremolo. The three lines are equivalent to the three beams connecting the notes in the 32nd-note rhythm. Therefore, the chart below indicates to tremolo pick the note in a 32nd-note rhythm for the duration of a whole note (four beats). Similarly, if a tremolo were indicated with only two lines above the whole note, then you would tremolo pick in a 16th-note rhythm for the duration of the whole note (four beats).

Play each note in the exercises below using tremolo picking. Practice tremolo picking of all the scales.

Ex. 75

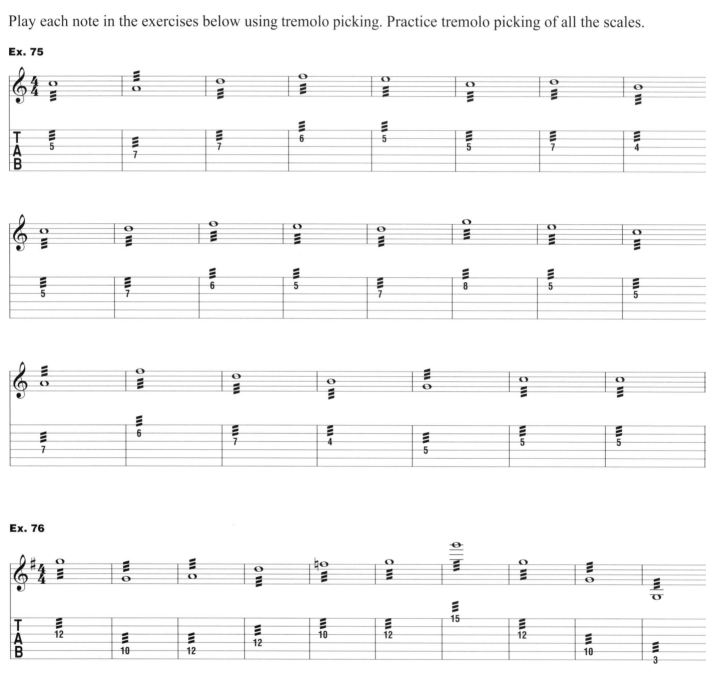

Ex. 76

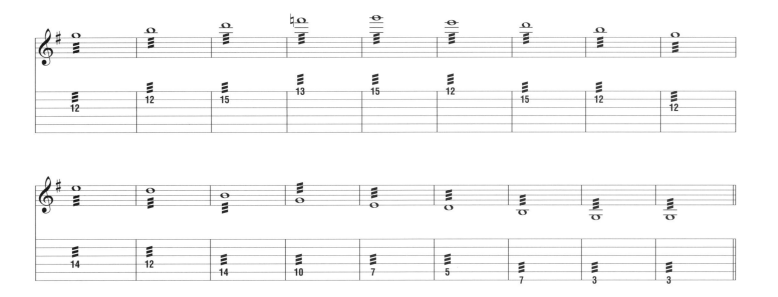

RIGHT HAND EXERCISES

The following exercise must be played in strict time. Play the first part slowly enough so that the exercise can be finished in the same tempo. While playing the slower notes at the beginning of the exercise, strive to get an exceptionally good, solid tone.

Ex. 77

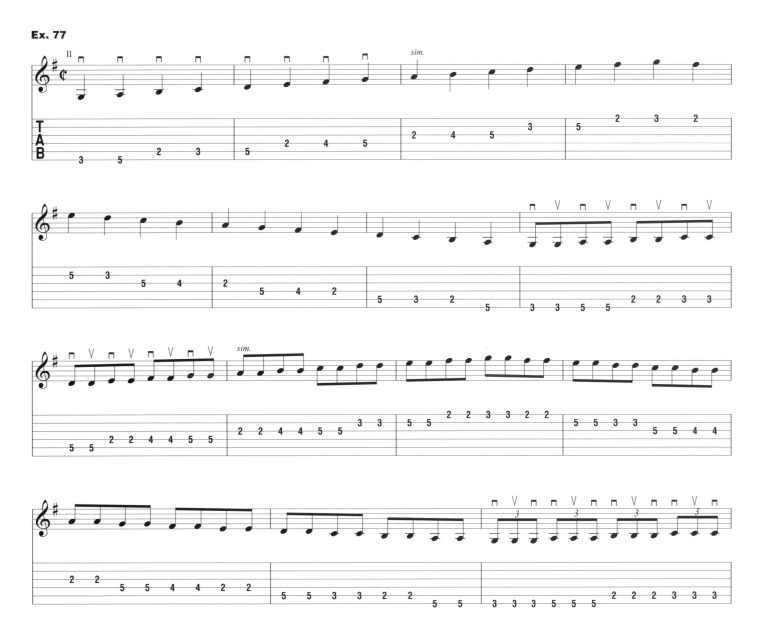

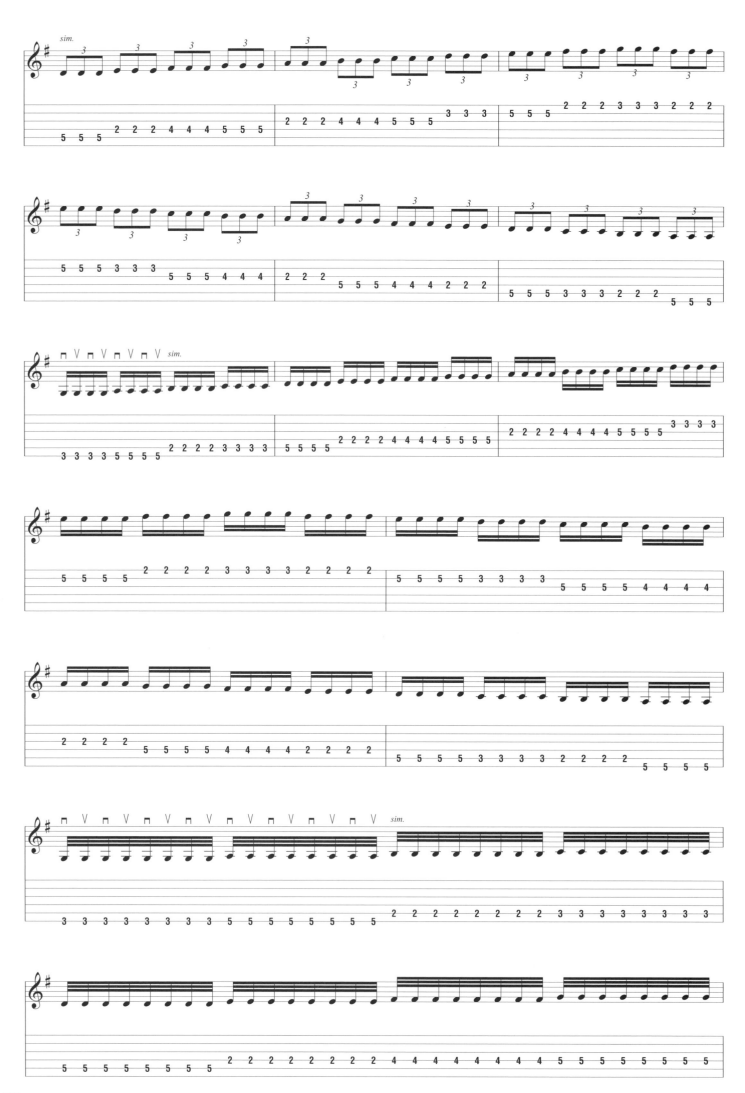

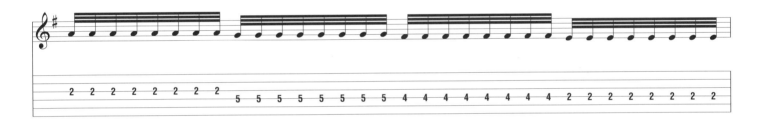

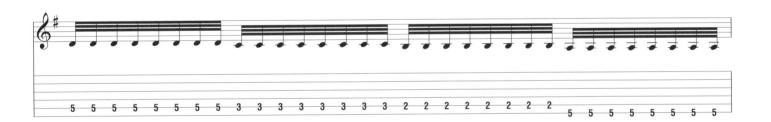

Ex. 78

Ex. 79

Ex. 80

FINGER CONTROL

Keep all fingers pressing down at the frets shown with black dots in the diagrams; move only the finger shown with a white dot while performing each exercise. Start slowly and work up to a tremolo, then slow down to stop.

Ex. 81

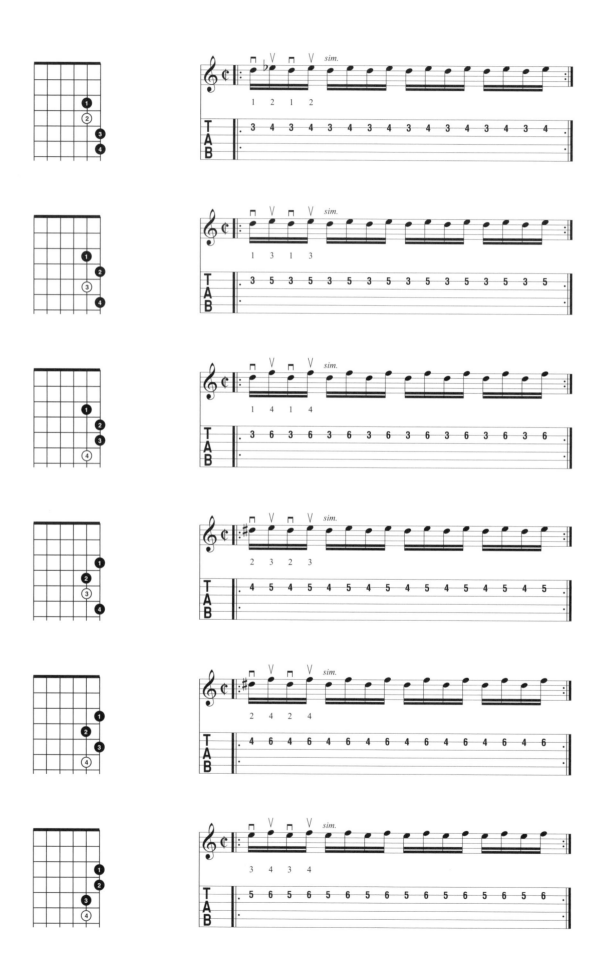

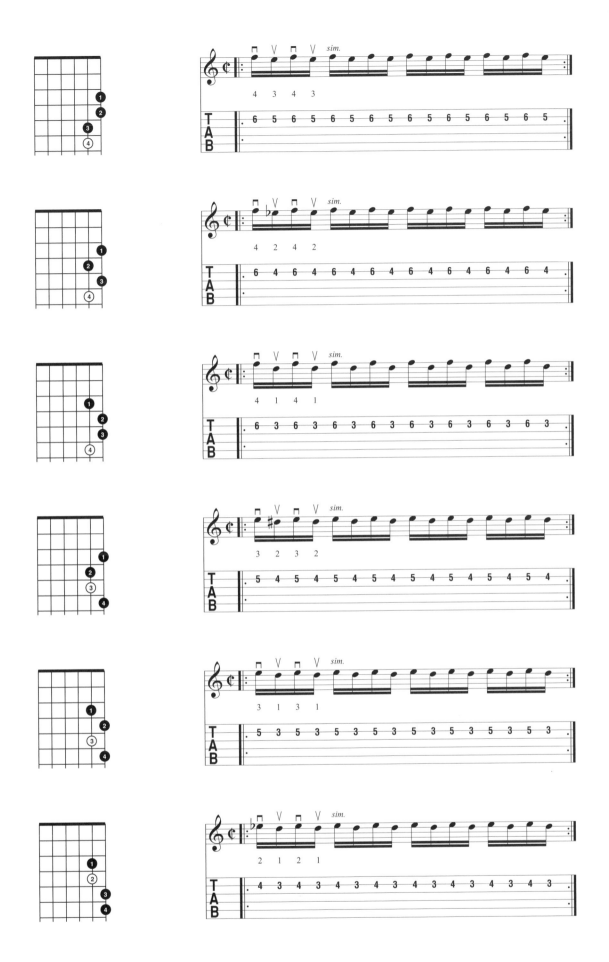

Once you've practiced these 12 exercises to the point where the tremolo is fast and even, use the same notes and work the fingers independently. Strive for coordination, continuity, and clarity in all tempos, between the two fingers in use as well as the left- and right-hand coordination.

TRIPLET STUDIES

Form a G chord.

Ex. 82

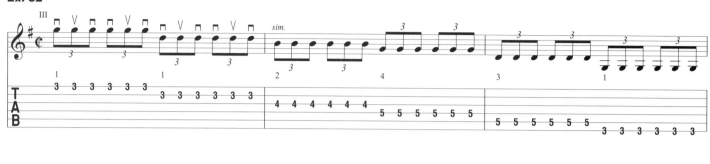

Ex. 83

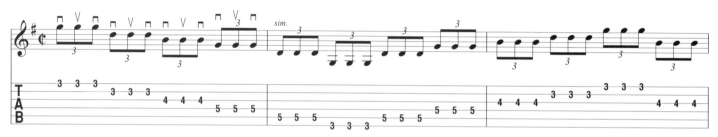

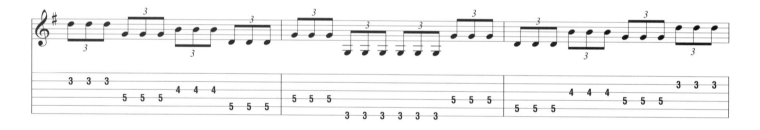

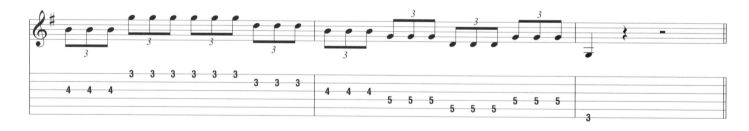

Ex. 84

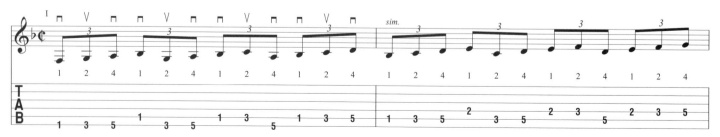

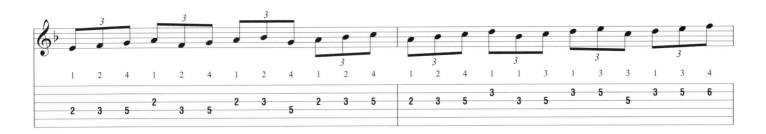

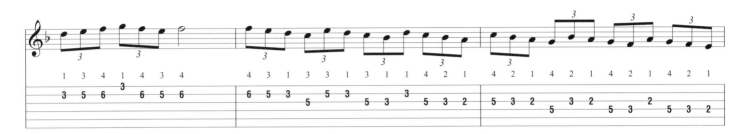

Ex. 85

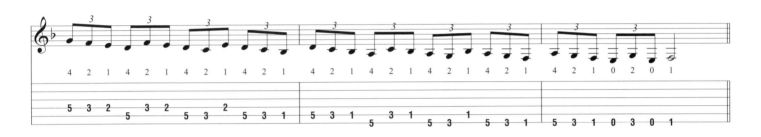

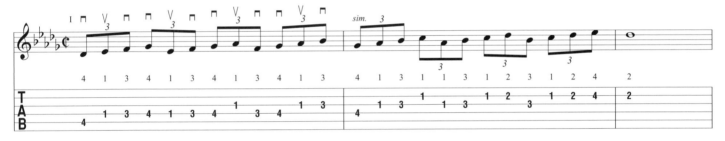

Ex. 86

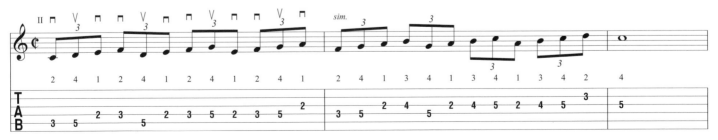

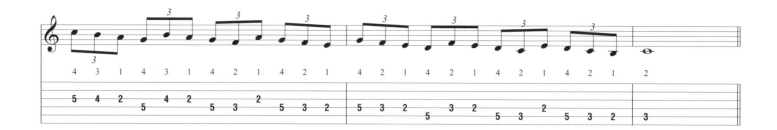

Ex. 87

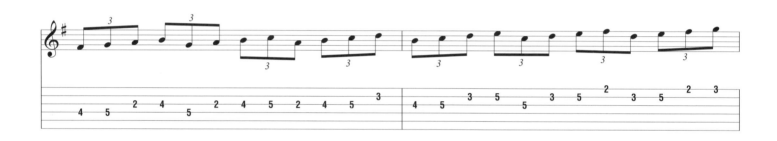

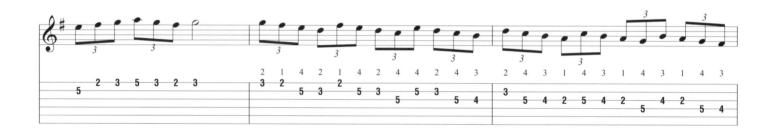

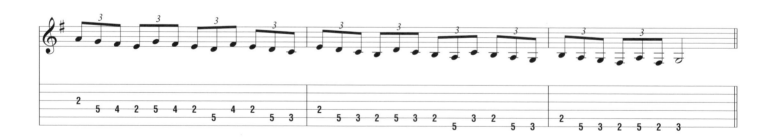

Ex. 88

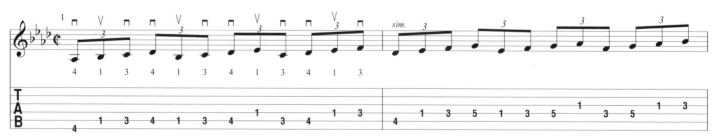

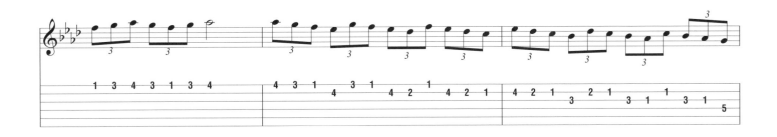

ACCENTS

An accent is performed by sharply picking the notes with accent marks (>) heavier than the other notes. Practice the following two examples chromatically up the fretboard.

Ex. 89

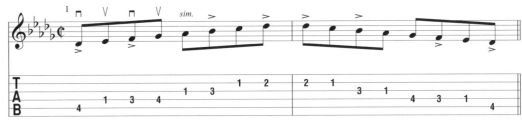

Ex. 90

Ex. 91

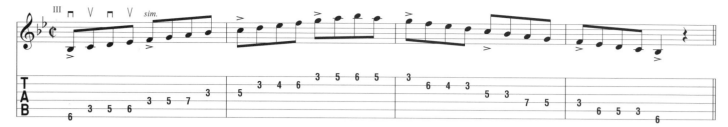

Ex. 92

Ex. 93

Ex. 94

Ex. 95

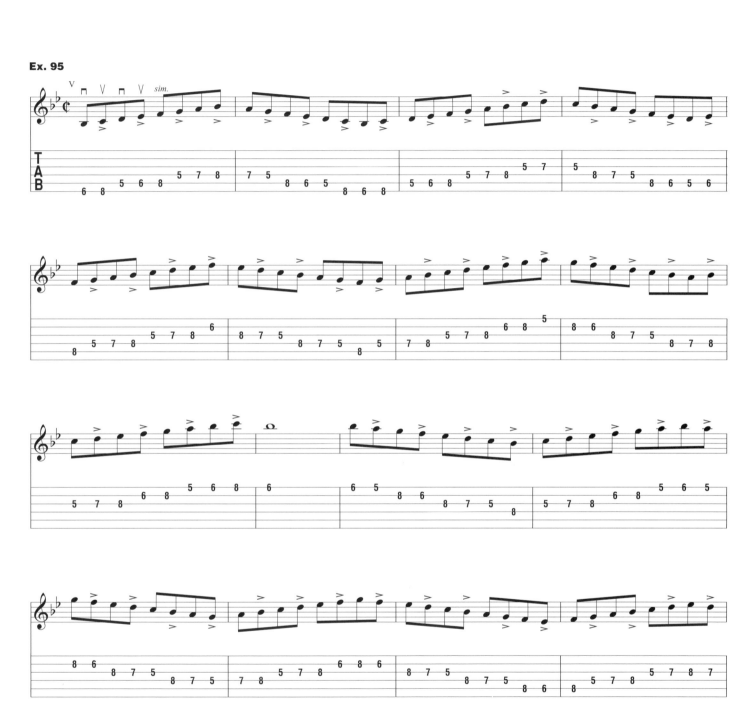

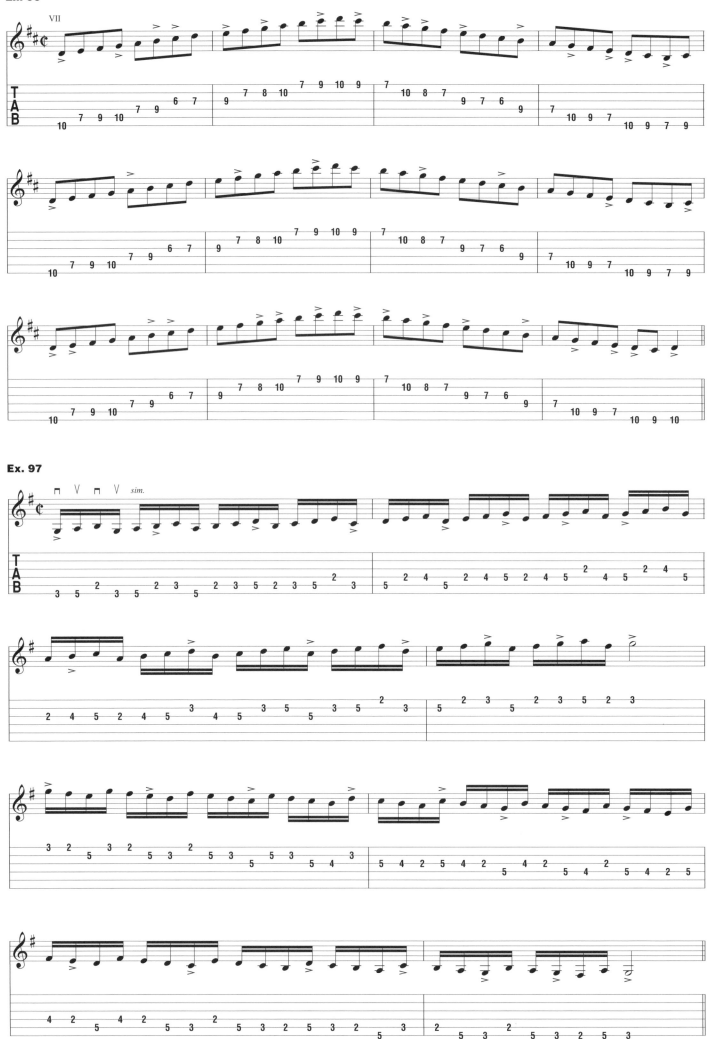

Ex. 97

Practice the previous exercise very carefully and thoroughly before attempting this next one. Play through it first without the accents to get the feel of it. Add the accents after you gain confidence. Play through it slowly at first in strict tempo.

Ex. 98

SYNCOPATION AND PICKING EXERCISES

Ex. 99

Ex. 100

NATURAL MINOR SCALES
(ONE OCTAVE)

Practice chromatically in all keys.

Ex. 101

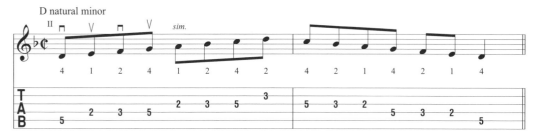

D natural minor

Ex. 102

Ex. 103

Ex. 104

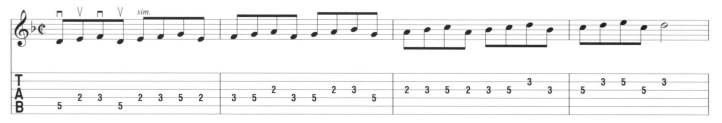

Ex. 106

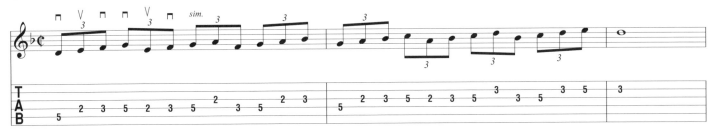

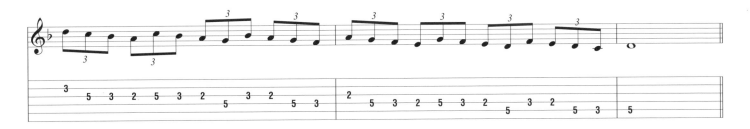

Practice chromatically in all keys.

Ex. 107

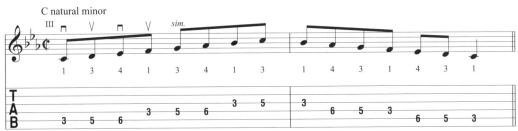

Ex. 108

Ex. 109

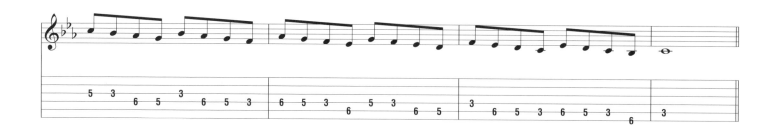

Ex. 110

Ex. 111

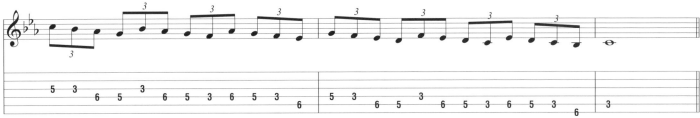

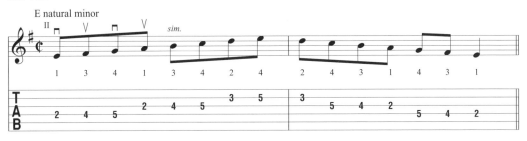

Practice chromatically in all keys.

Ex. 113

Ex. 114

Ex. 115

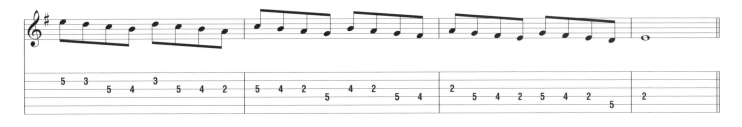

Ex. 116

Ex. 117

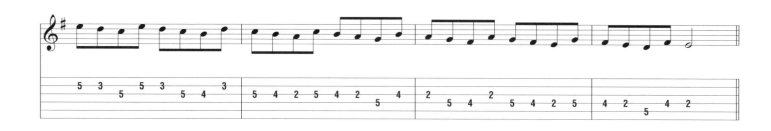

Ex. 118

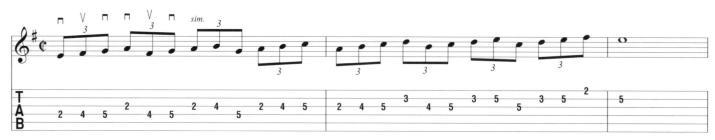

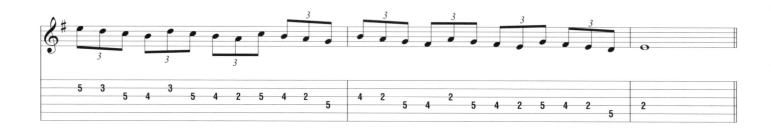

TWO OCTAVE NATURAL MINOR SCALES

Practice chromatically in all keys.

Ex. 119

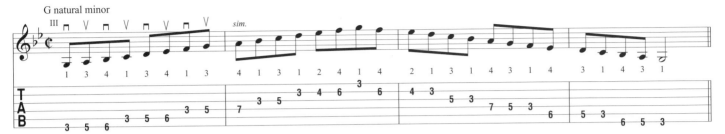

Ex. 120

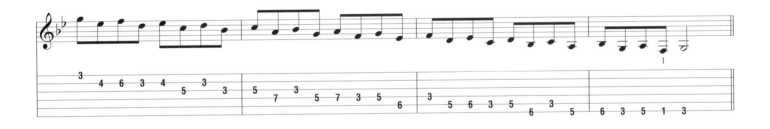

Ex. 121

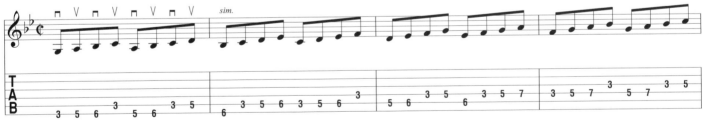

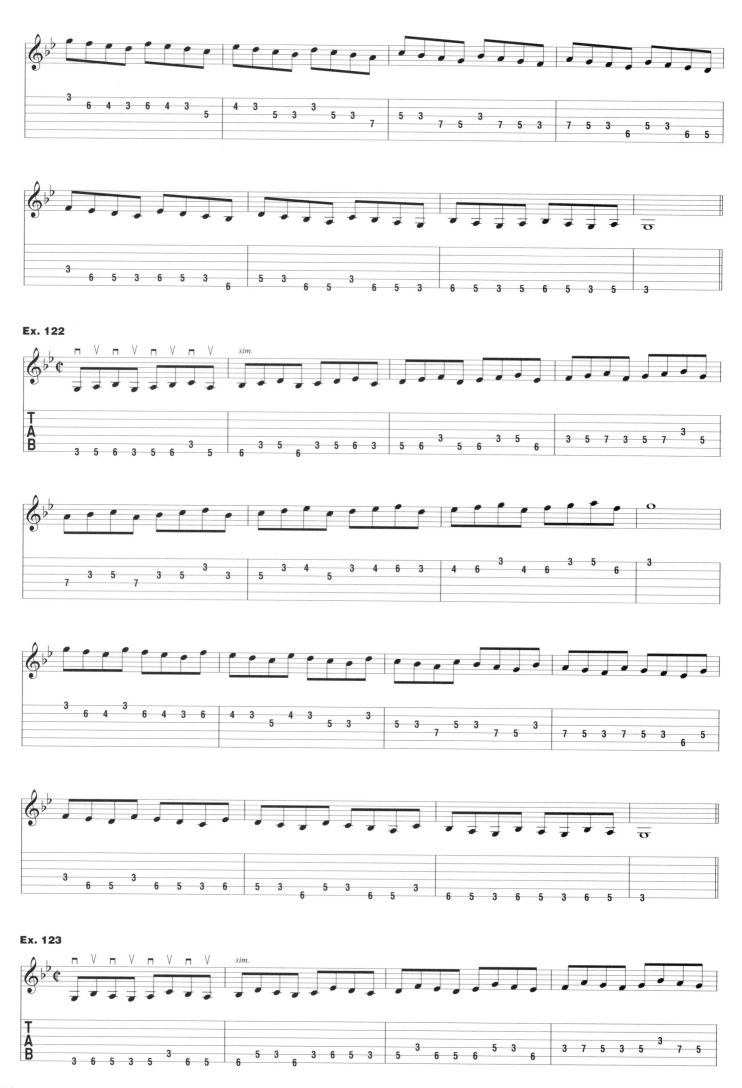

Ex. 122

Ex. 123

Ex. 124

Practice chromatically in all keys.

Ex. 125

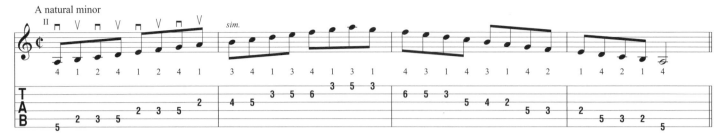

Ex. 126

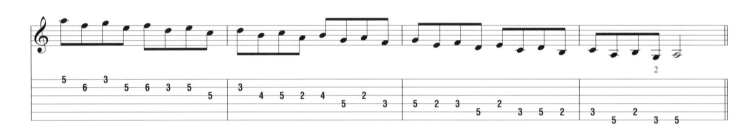

Ex. 127

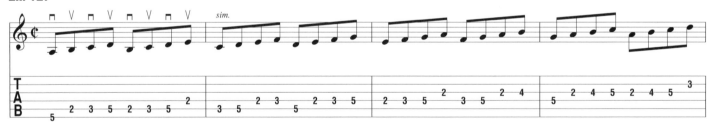

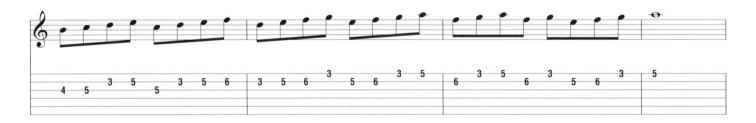

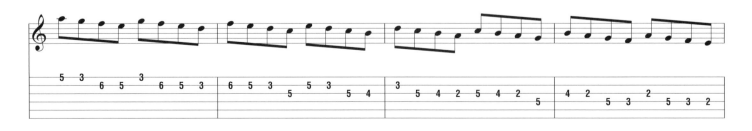

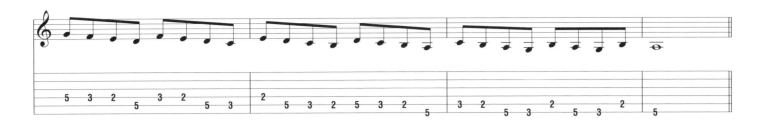

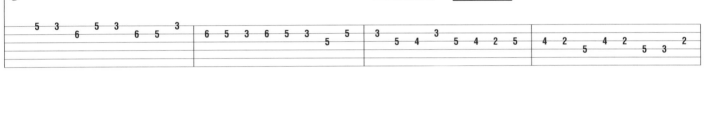

Ex. 128

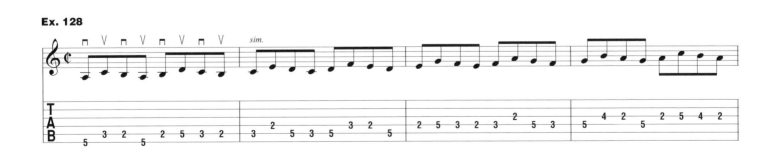

Ex. 130

Practice chromatically in all keys.

Ex. 131

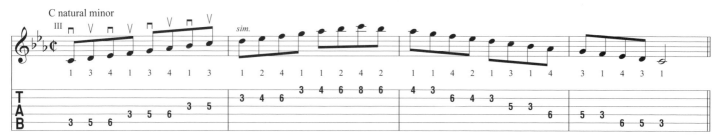

Ex. 132

Ex. 133

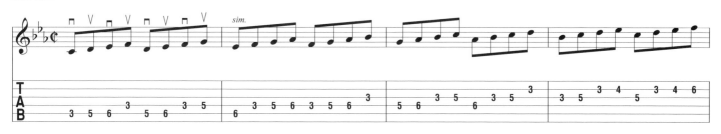

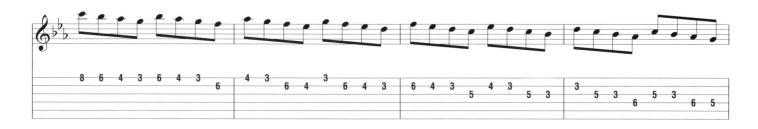

Ex. 134

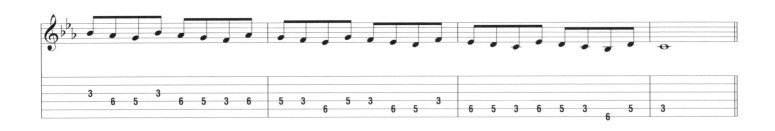

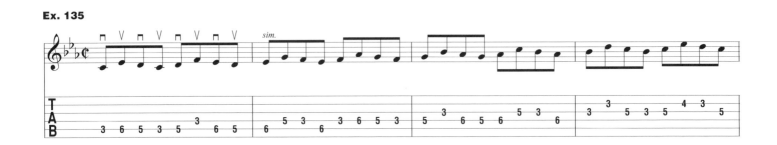

Ex. 135

Ex. 136

ALTERED MINOR SCALES

HARMONIC MINOR SCALES (ONE OCTAVE)

Ex. 137

E harmonic minor

Ex. 138

C harmonic minor

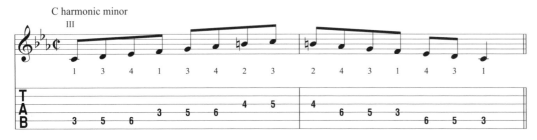

Ex. 139

D harmonic minor

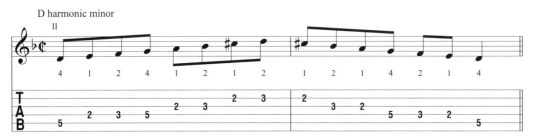

MELODIC MINOR SCALES (ONE OCTAVE)

Ex. 140

E melodic minor

Ex. 141

Ex. 142

JAZZ MELODIC MINOR SCALES (ONE OCTAVE)

Ex. 143

Ex. 144

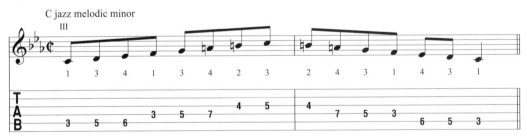

Ex. 145

EXTENDED ALTERED MINOR SCALES

Ex. 146

G harmonic minor

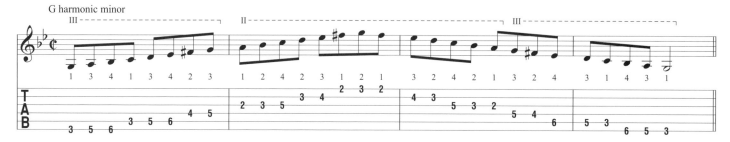

Ex. 147

G melodic minor

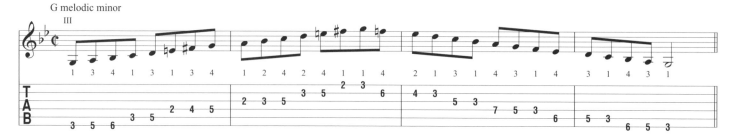

G melodic minor (alternate fingering)

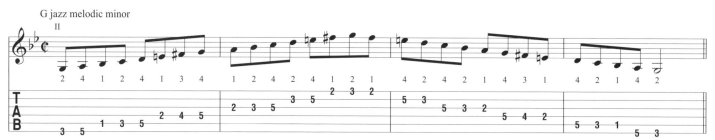

Ex. 148

G jazz melodic minor

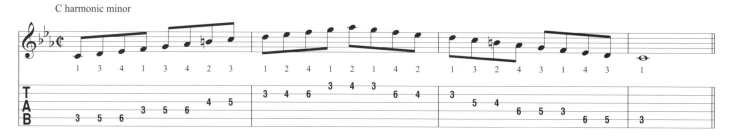

Ex. 149

C harmonic minor

Ex. 150

C melodic minor

Ex. 151

C jazz melodic minor

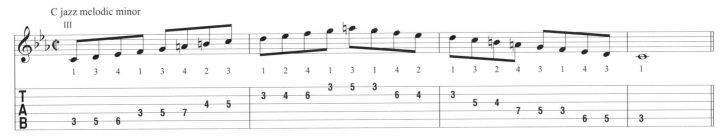

Ex. 152

A harmonic minor

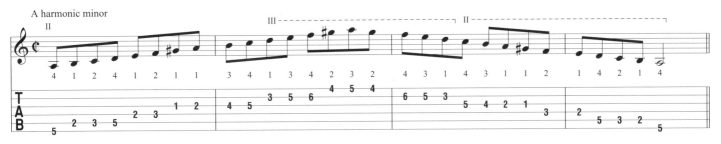

Ex. 153

A melodic minor

Ex. 154

A jazz melodic minor

ALTERED MINOR SCALE VARIATIONS

G harmonic minor

Ex. 155

Ex. 156

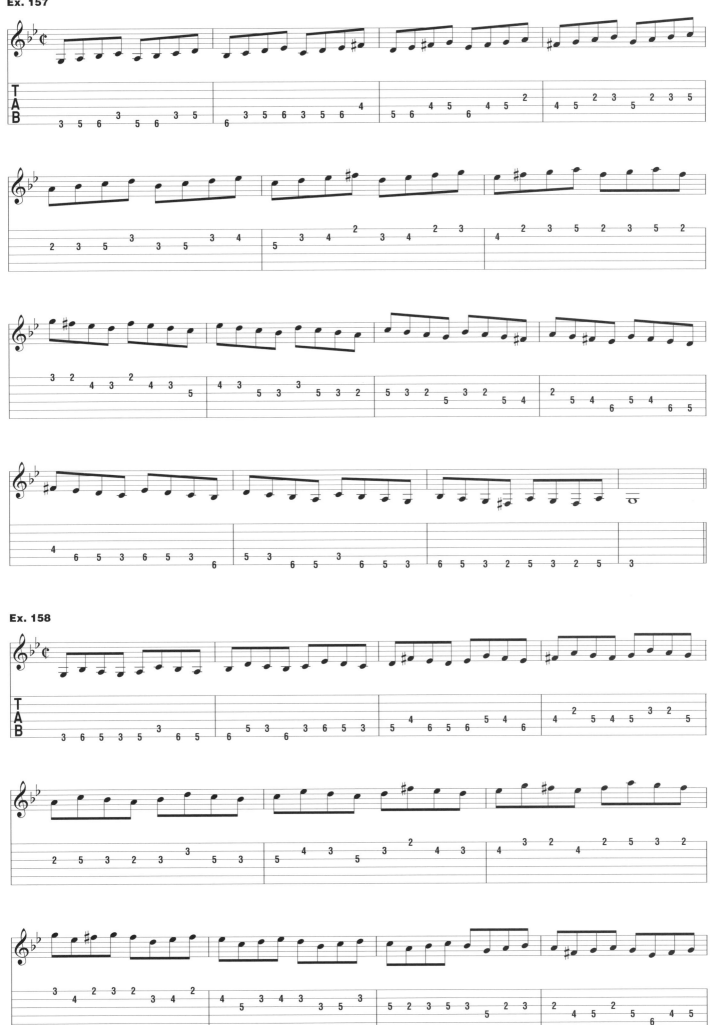

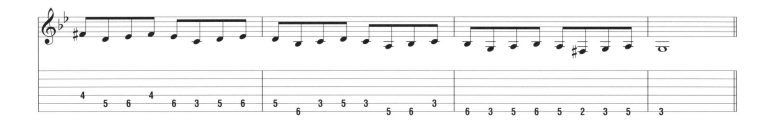

G melodic minor

Ex. 159

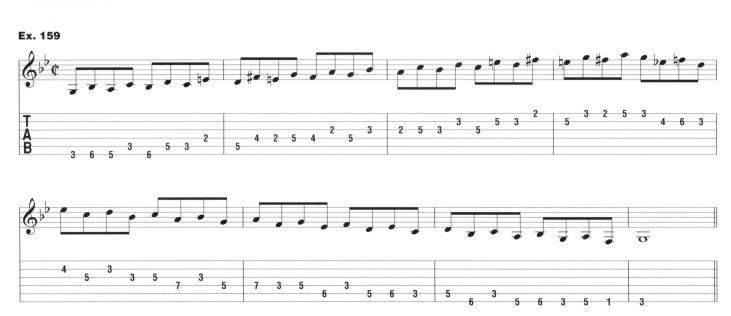

Ex. 160

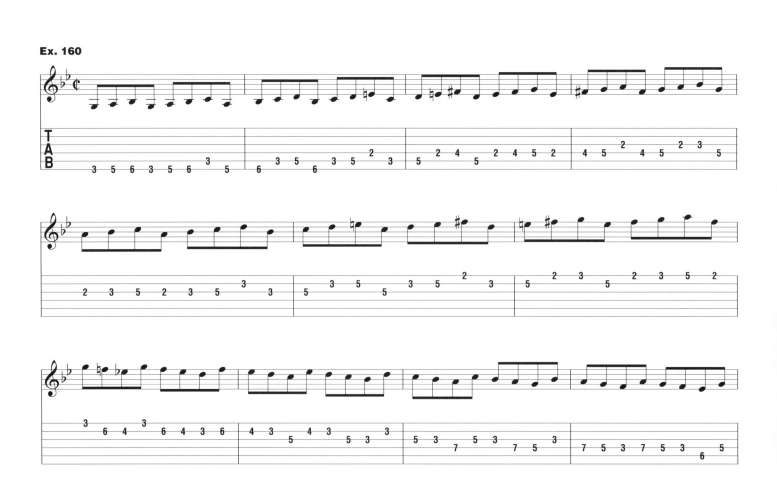

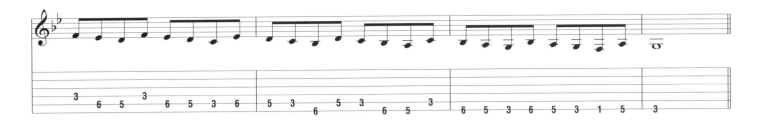

Ex. 161

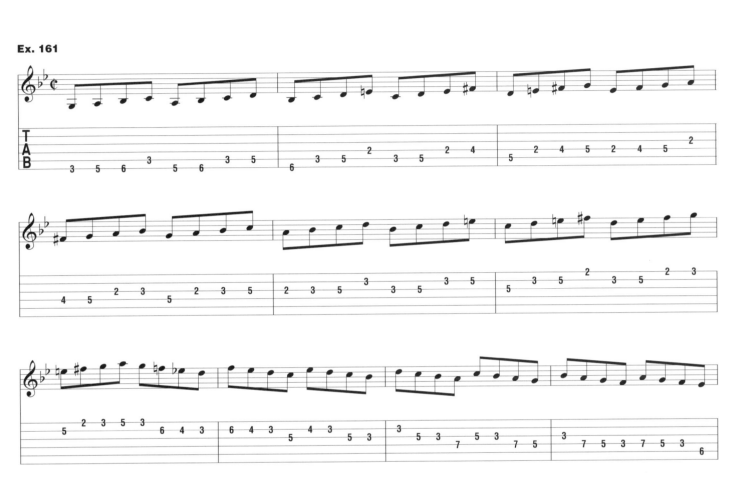

Ex. 162

G jazz melodic minor

Ex. 163

Ex. 164

Ex. 165

Ex. 166

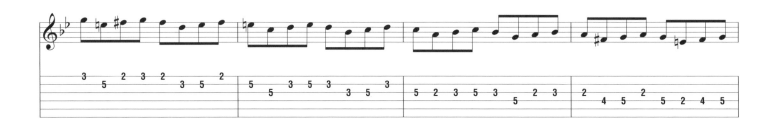

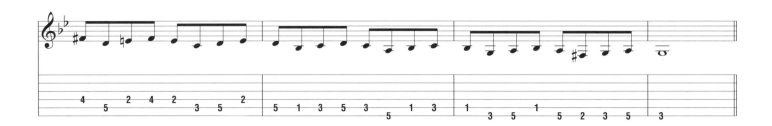

C harmonic minor

Ex. 167

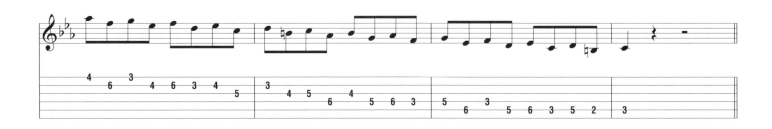

Ex. 168

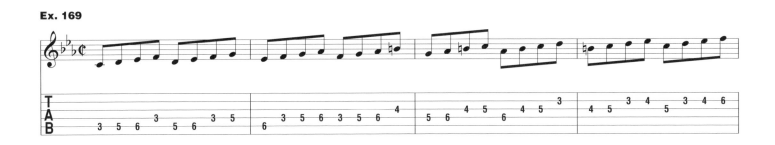

Ex. 169

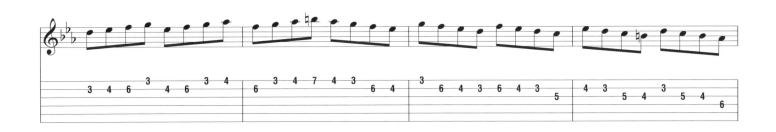

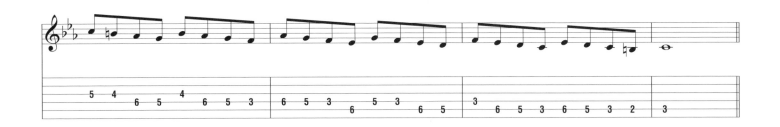

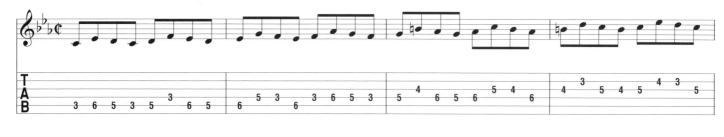

C melodic minor

Ex. 171

Ex. 172

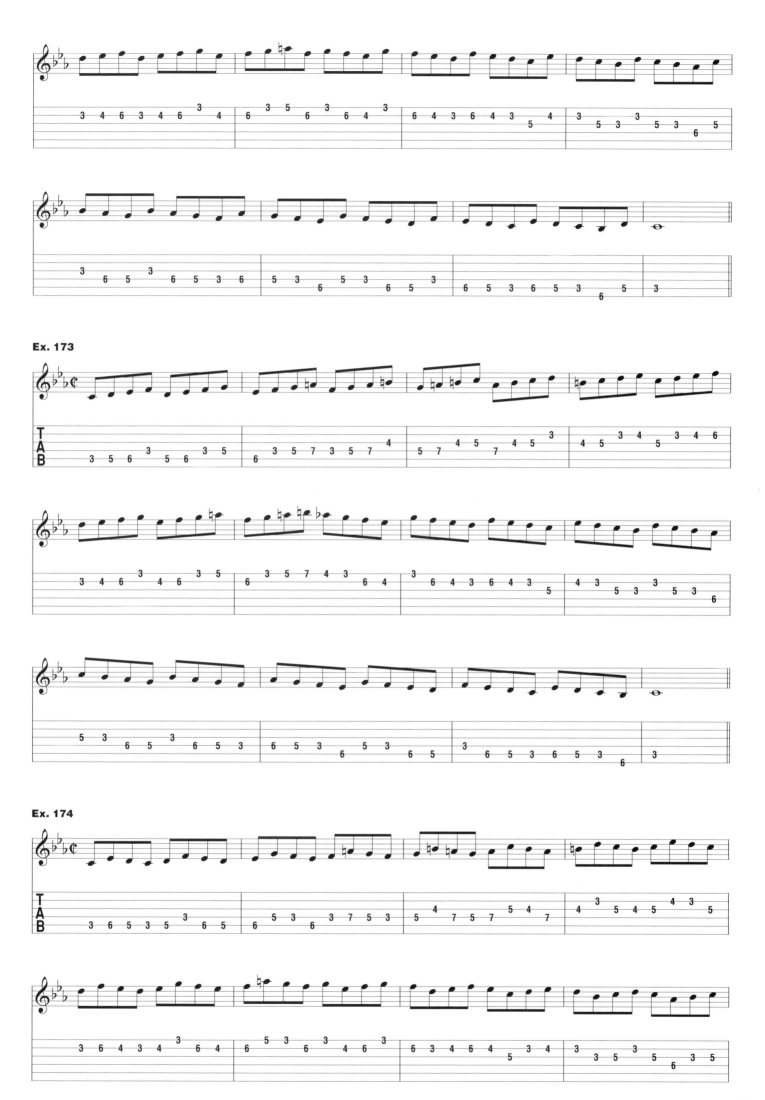

Ex. 173

Ex. 174

C jazz melodic minor

Ex. 175

Ex. 176

Ex. 177

Ex. 178

A harmonic minor

Ex. 179

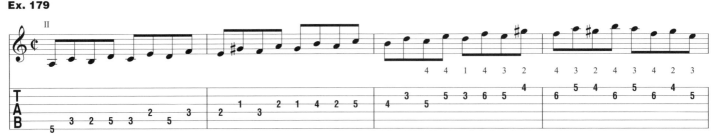

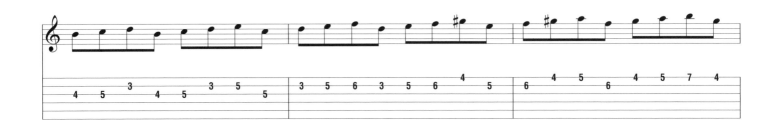

Ex. 180

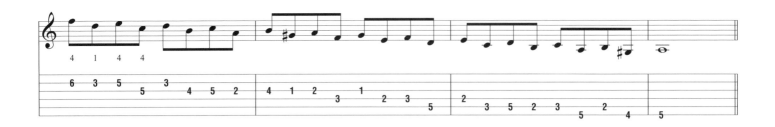

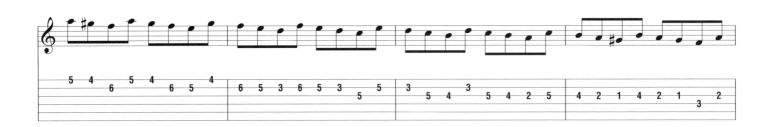

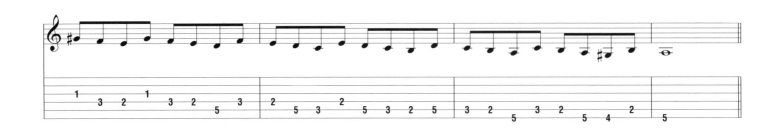

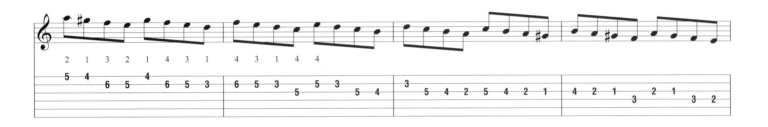

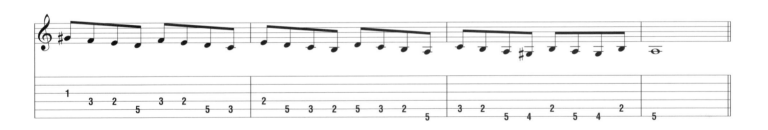

Ex. 182

A melodic minor

Ex. 183

Ex. 184

Ex. 185

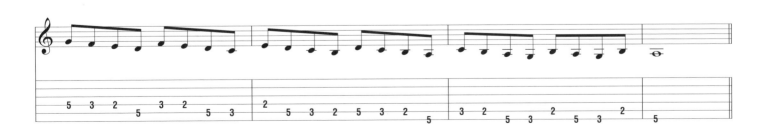

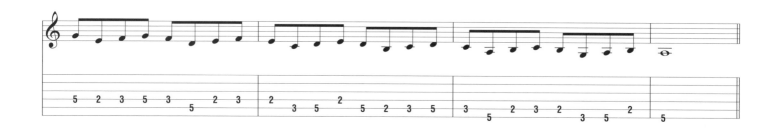

A jazz melodic minor

Ex. 187

Ex. 189

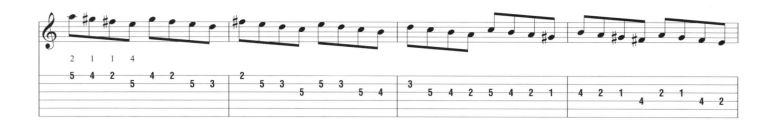

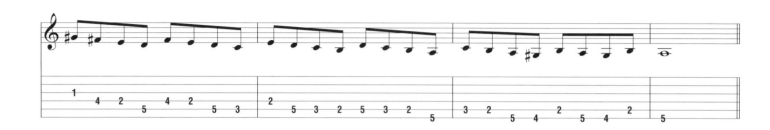

Ex. 190

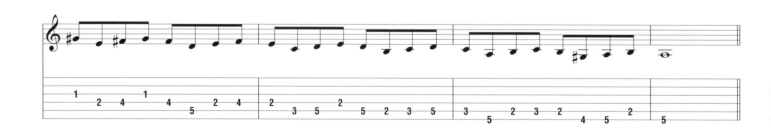

HARMONIC MINOR SCALE
AND VARIATIONS

Ex. 191

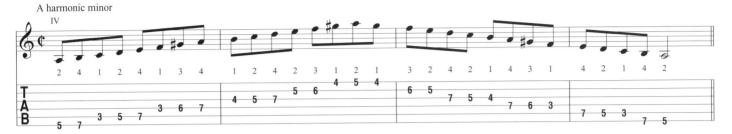

Ex. 192

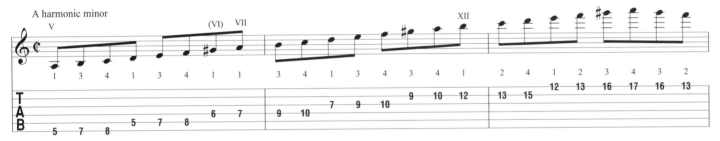

Ex. 193

Ex. 194

Ex. 195

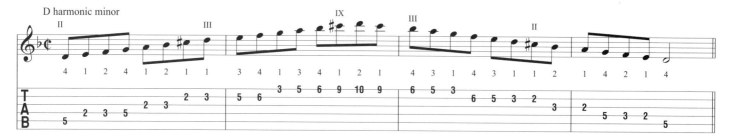

Ex. 196

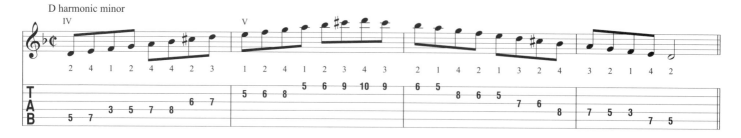

Ex. 197

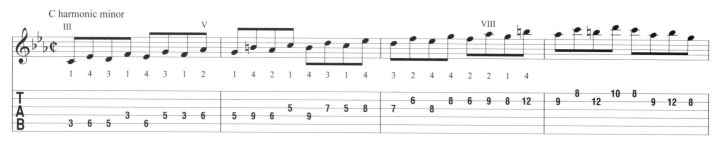

Ex. 198

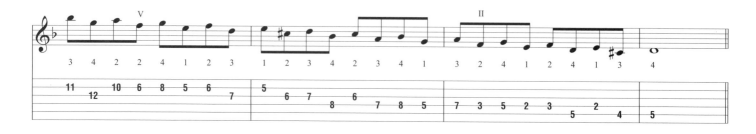

Ex. 199

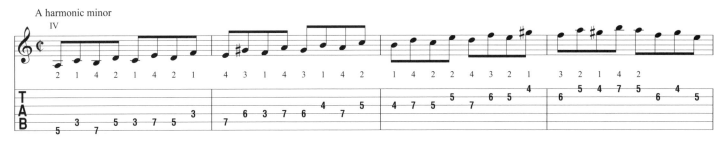

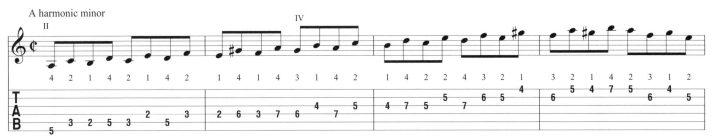

Ex. 200

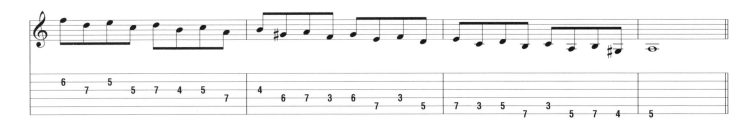

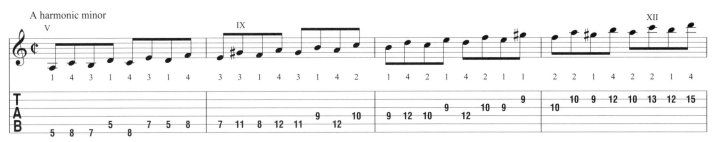

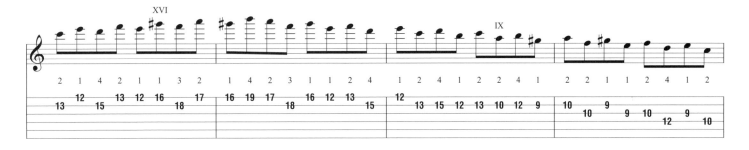

Ex. 201

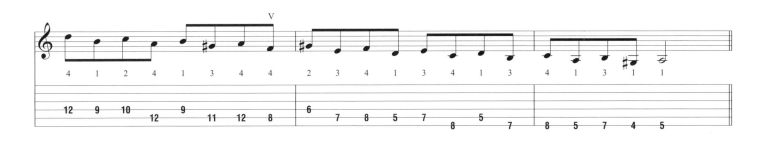

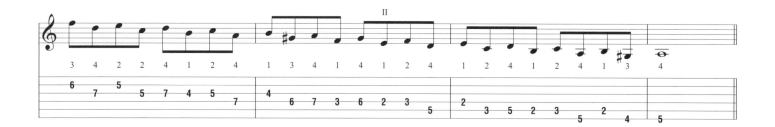

Ex. 202

A harmonic minor

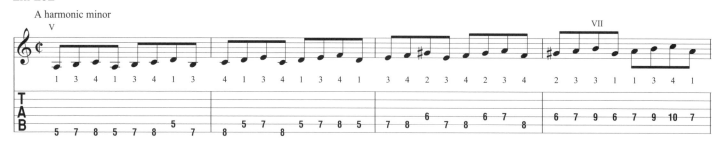

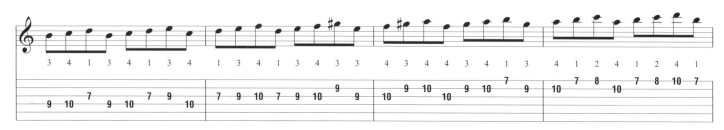

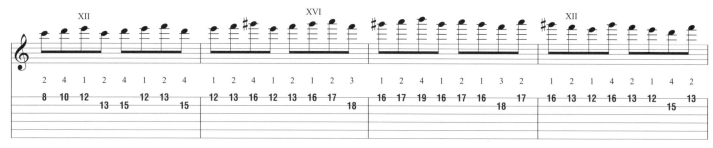

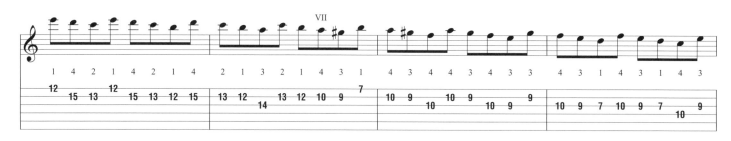

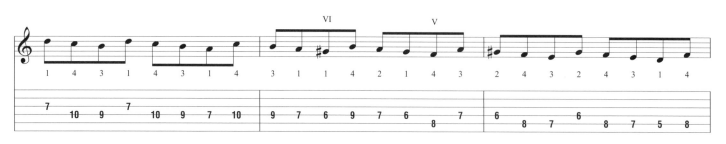

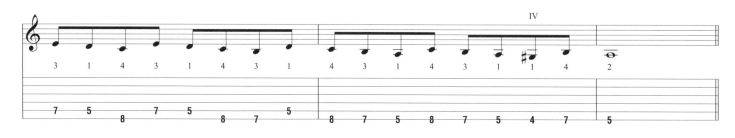

Ex. 203

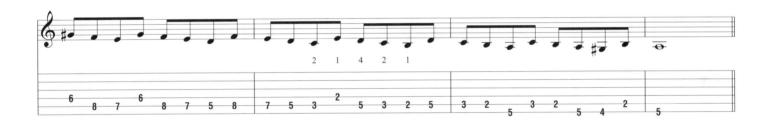

Ex. 204

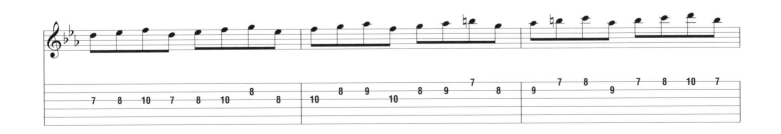

Ex. 205

D harmonic minor

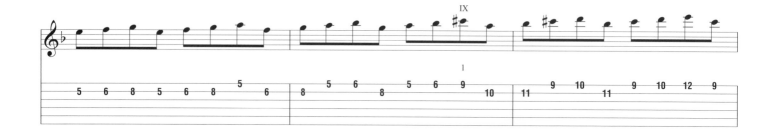

Ex. 206

A harmonic minor

MELODIC MINOR SCALE AND VARIATIONS

Ex. 207

Ex. 208

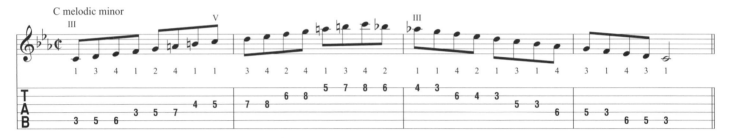

Ex. 209

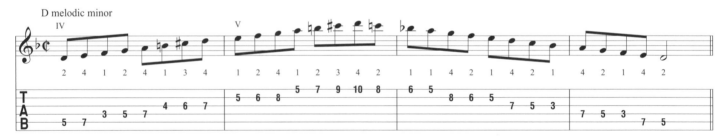

Ex. 210

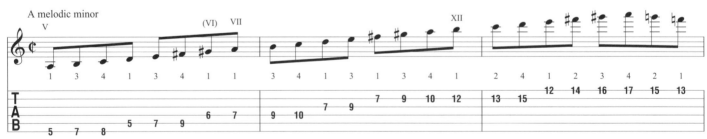

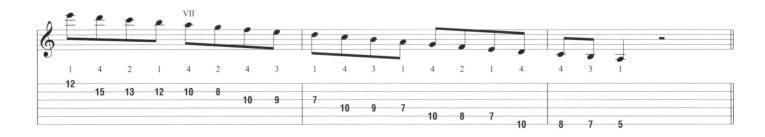

Ex. 211

Ex. 212

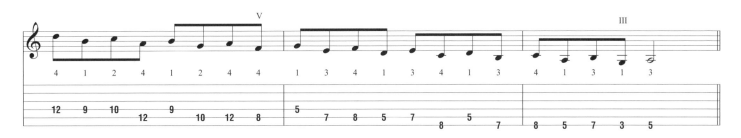

Ex. 213

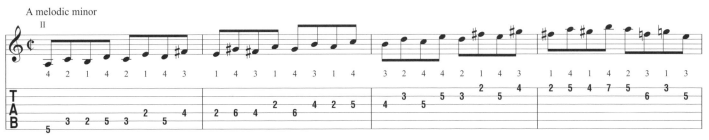

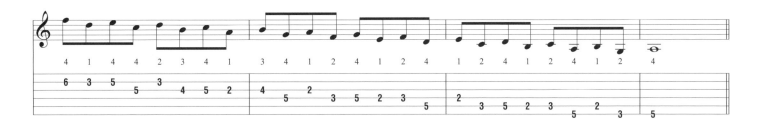

Ex. 214

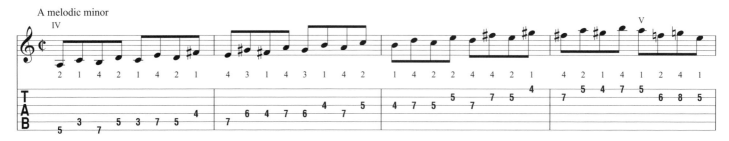

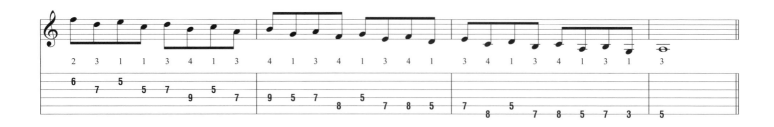

Ex. 215

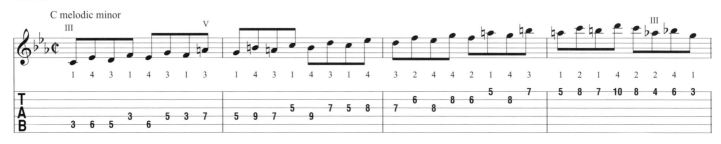

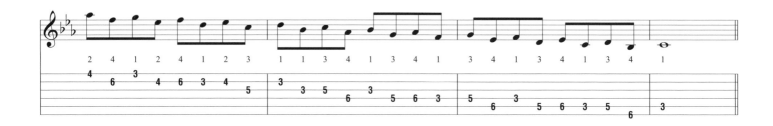

Ex. 216

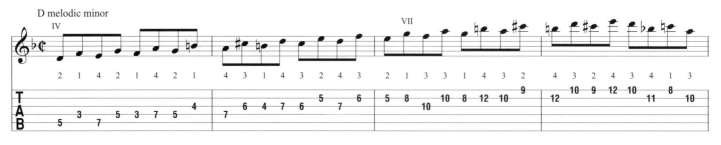

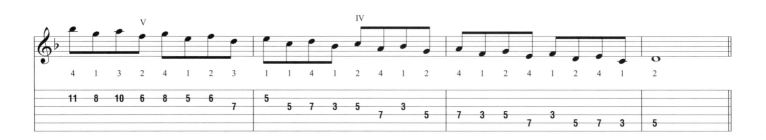

Ex. 217

A melodic minor

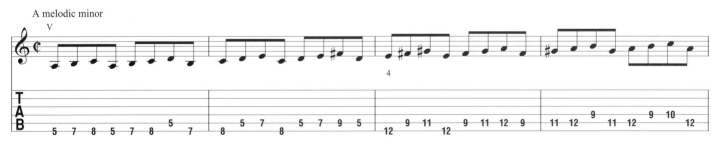

Ex. 218

A melodic minor

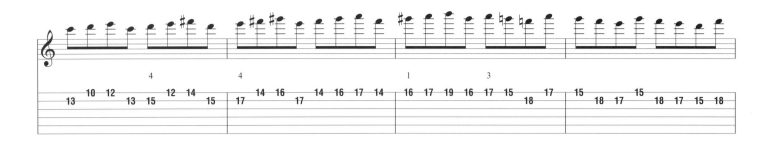

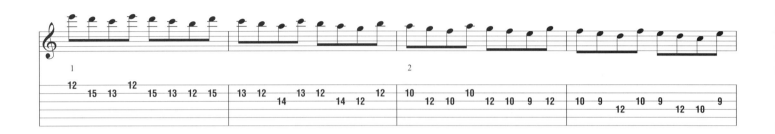

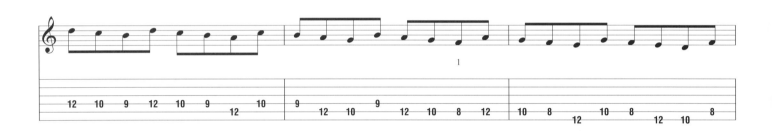

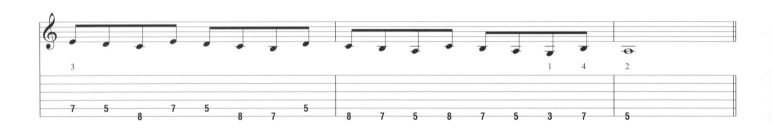

Ex. 219

Ex. 220

C melodic minor

Ex. 221

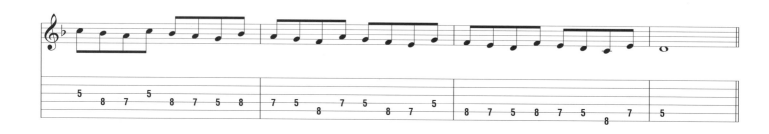

JAZZ MELODIC MINOR SCALE AND VARIATIONS

Ex. 222

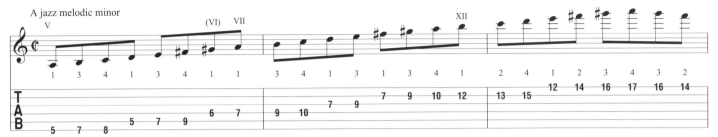

Ex. 223

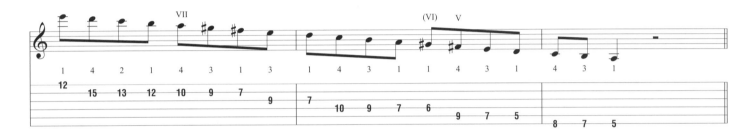

Ex. 224

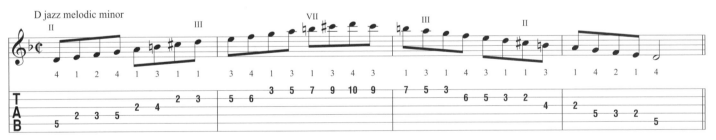

Ex. 225

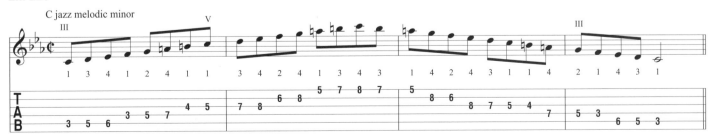

Ex. 226

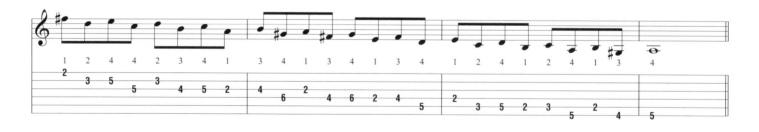

Ex. 227

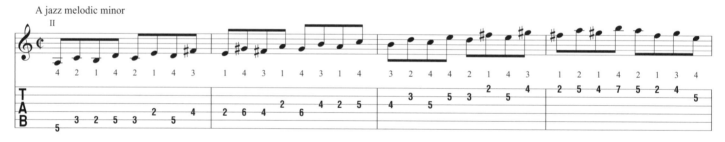

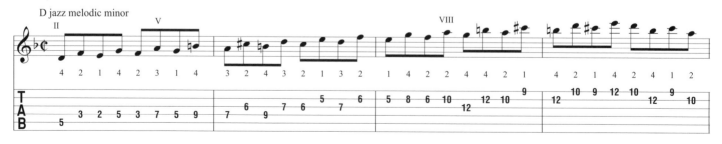

Ex. 228

Ex. 229

Ex. 230

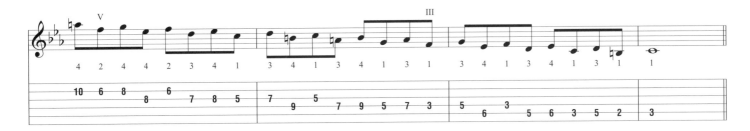

Ex. 231

Ex. 232

A jazz melodic minor

Ex. 233

A jazz melodic minor

Ex. 234

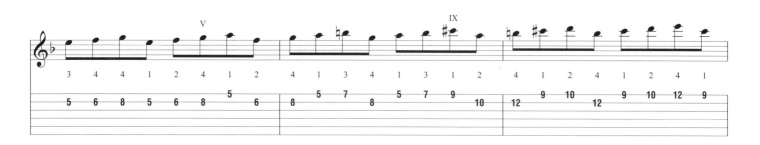

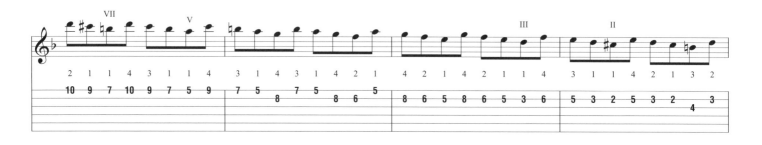

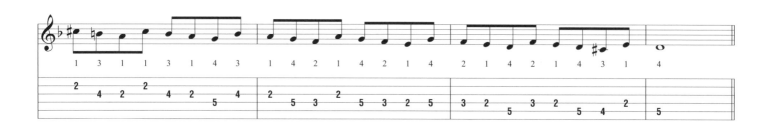

Ex. 235

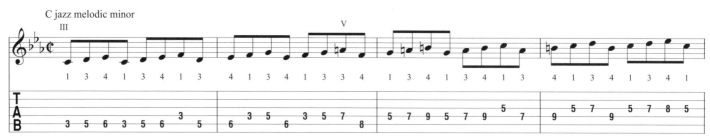

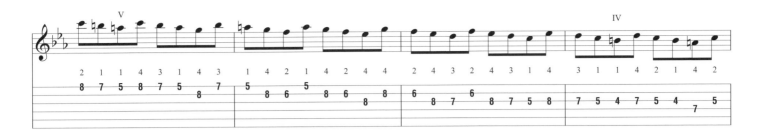

JAZZ MELODIC MINOR SCALES IN LONG FORM

Ex. 236

A jazz melodic minor

Ex. 237

D jazz melodic minor

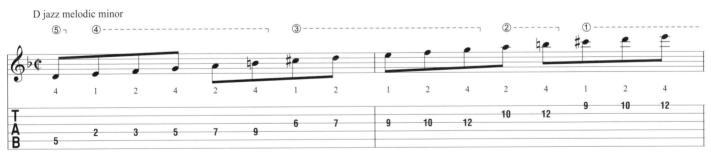

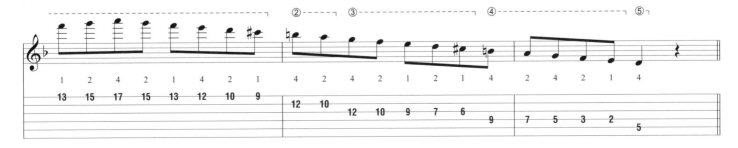

Ex. 238

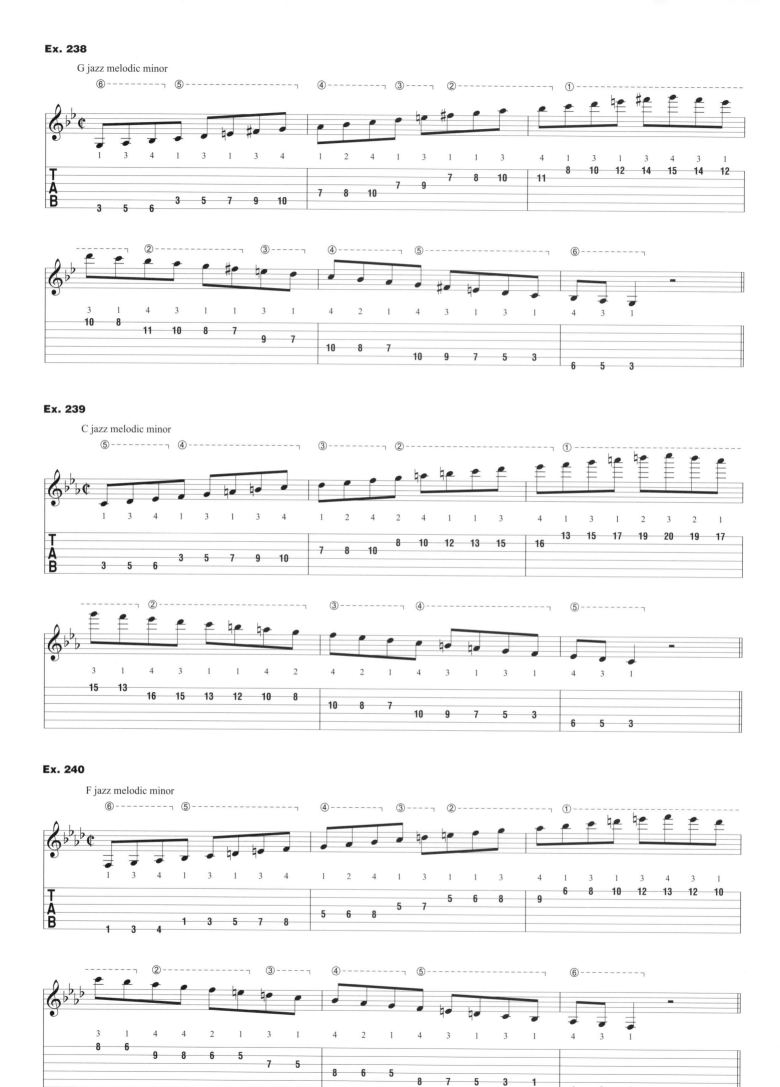

Ex. 239

Ex. 240

Ex. 241

B♭ jazz melodic minor

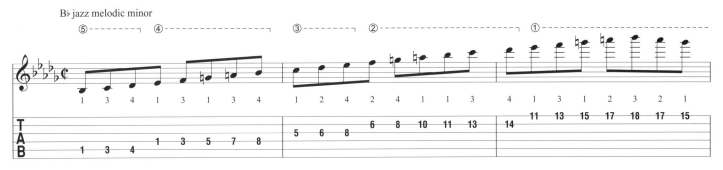

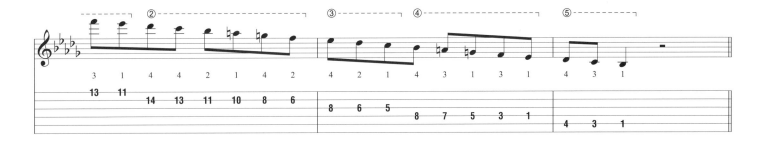

Ex. 242

E♭ jazz melodic minor

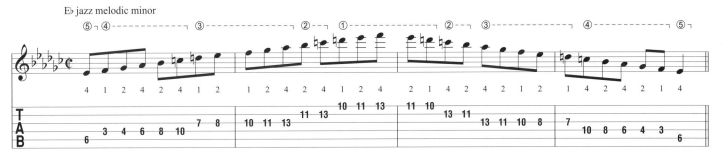

Ex. 243

G♯ jazz melodic minor

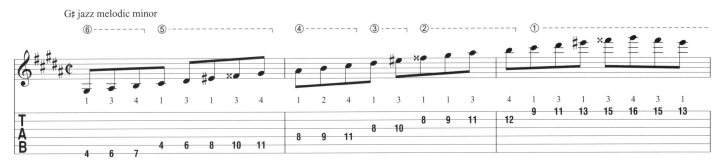

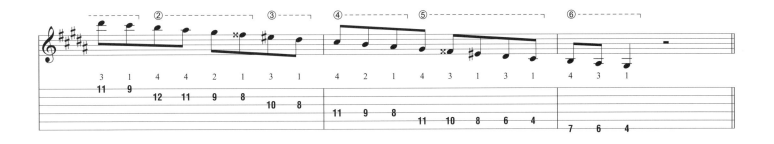

Ex. 244

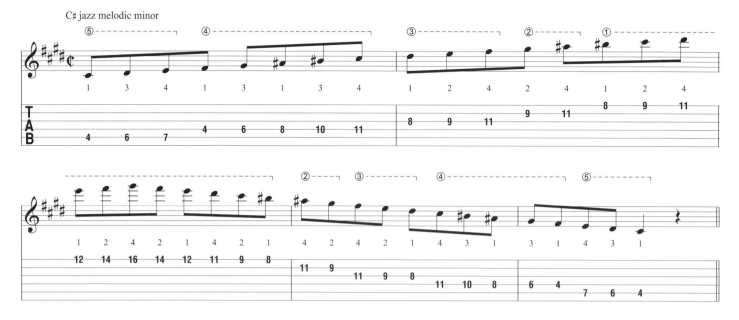

Ex. 245

Ex. 246

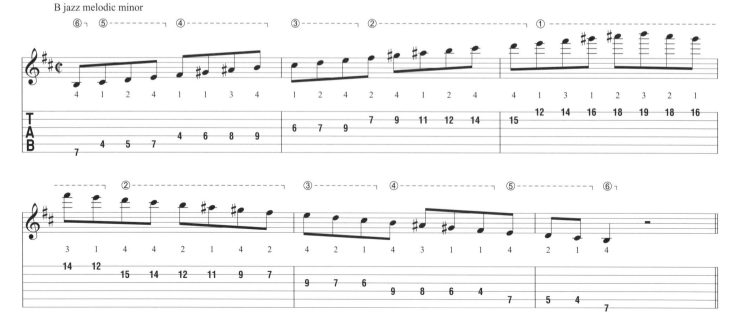

Ex. 247

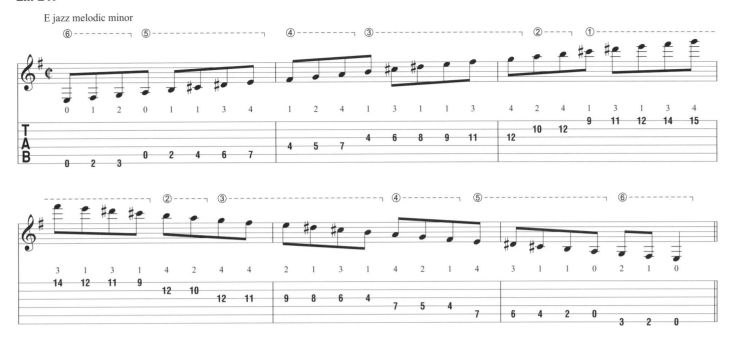

WHOLE TONE SCALES

The whole tone scale is made up entirely of consecutive whole steps. Basically, there are only two scales: the C and the D♭ whole tone scales. The rest of them are derived from those two.

Play these scales using the same treatment and patterns as was done with the major scales.

Ex. 248

Ex. 249

Ex. 250

F whole tone

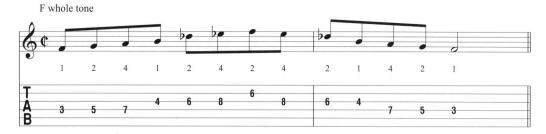

Ex. 251

A♯ whole tone

Ex. 252

E♭ whole tone

Ex. 253

A♭ whole tone

Ex. 254

G♭ whole tone

128

Ex. 255

B whole tone

Ex. 256

E whole tone

Ex. 257

A whole tone

Ex. 258

D whole tone

Ex. 259

G whole tone

PENTATONIC SCALES

MAJOR PENTATONIC SCALES

Made up of the 1st, 2nd, 3rd, 5th, and 6th steps of the major scale.

Ex. 260

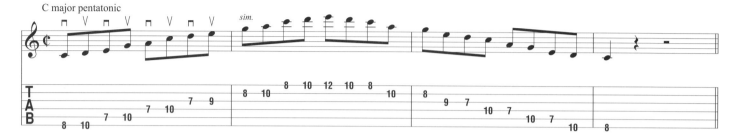

Ex. 261

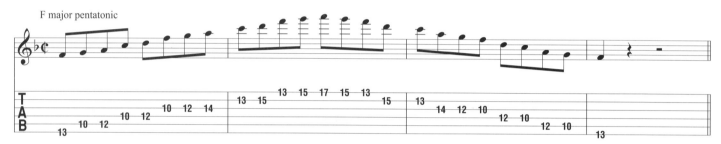

Ex. 262

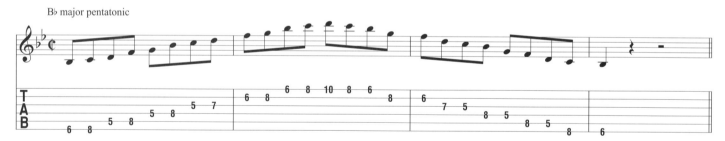

MINOR PENTATONIC SCALES

Made up of the 1st, ♭3rd, 4th, 5th, and ♭7th steps of the minor scale.

Ex. 263

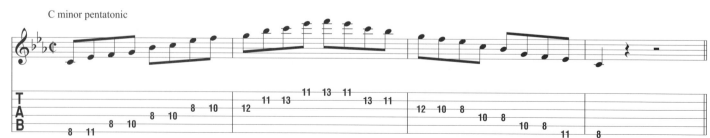

Ex. 264

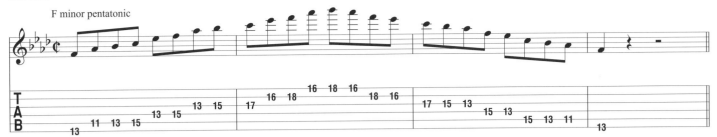

Ex. 265

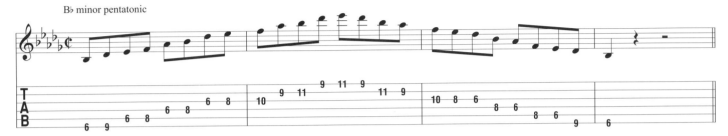

Play in all keys.

MORE TECHNICAL EXERCISES

PICK CONTROL

There are two ways to play the following examples: normal and sustained. To play normally, lift each finger after playing a note, just enough to stop the note from ringing as the next note is struck. To play sustained, leave all fingers down fretting the notes so that all notes ring out (like when a sustain pedal is held down on a piano). While picking, do not separate the strokes; draw the pick over the strings evenly. Try to keep the pick straight and parallel to the strings—not slanted in either direction. Practice all examples chromatically up the fretboard.

Ex. 266

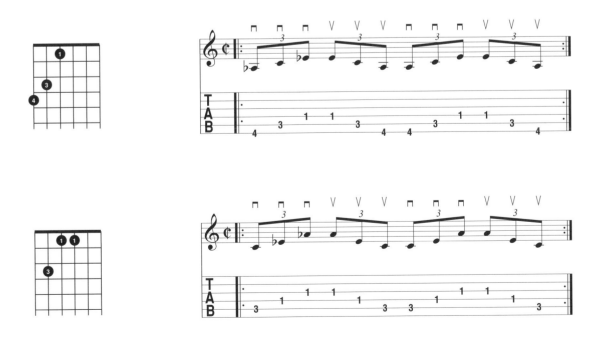

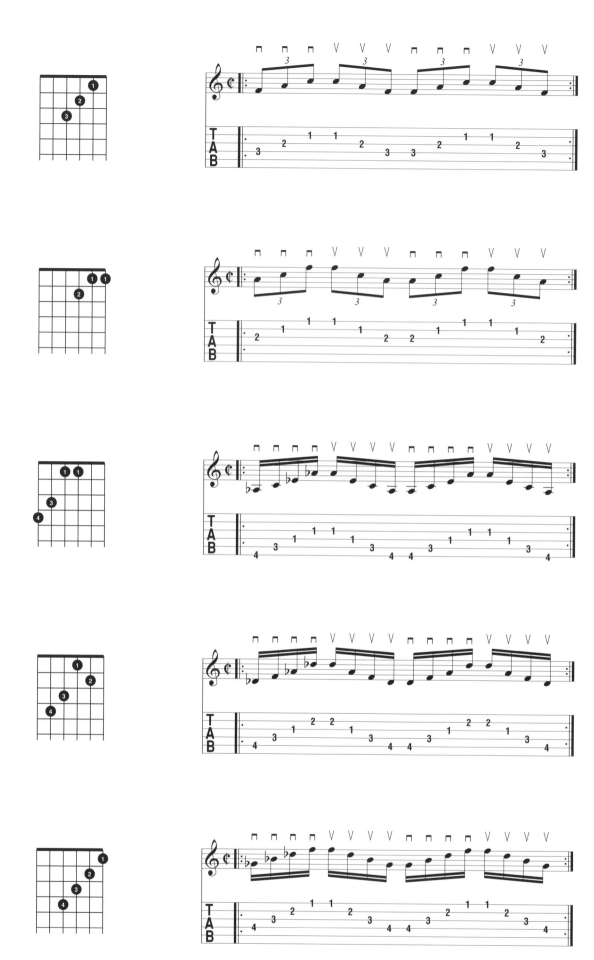

FINGER CONTROL AND PICK CONTROL

Fingering

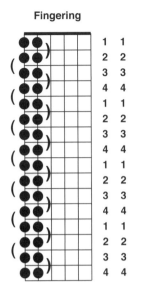

First practice this exercise with picking no. 1 (strict alternate picking) and then with picking no. 2 (sweeping across the strings). Take care with picking no. 2 to pick without separating the strokes—draw the pick evenly over the two strings. Try to keep the pick parallel to the strings instead of at an angle.

After playing the exercise both ways on the fifth and sixth strings, move it up to the fourth and fifth strings, then the third and fourth strings, and so on.

Ex. 267

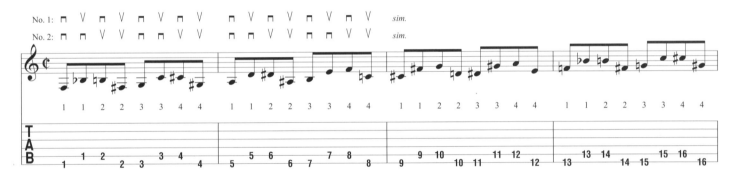

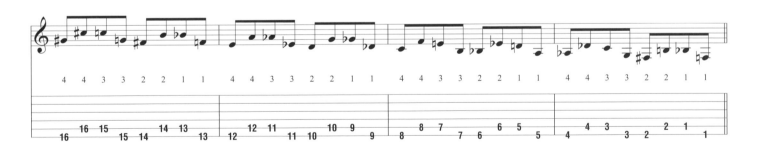

PREPARATION FOR THE SLUR

Ex. 268

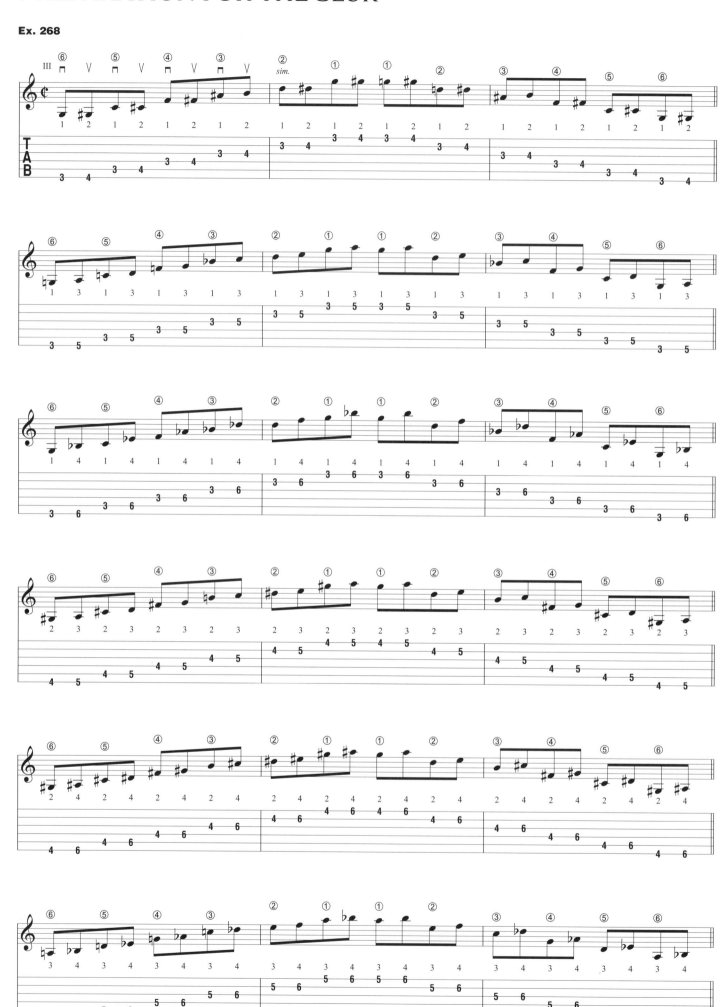

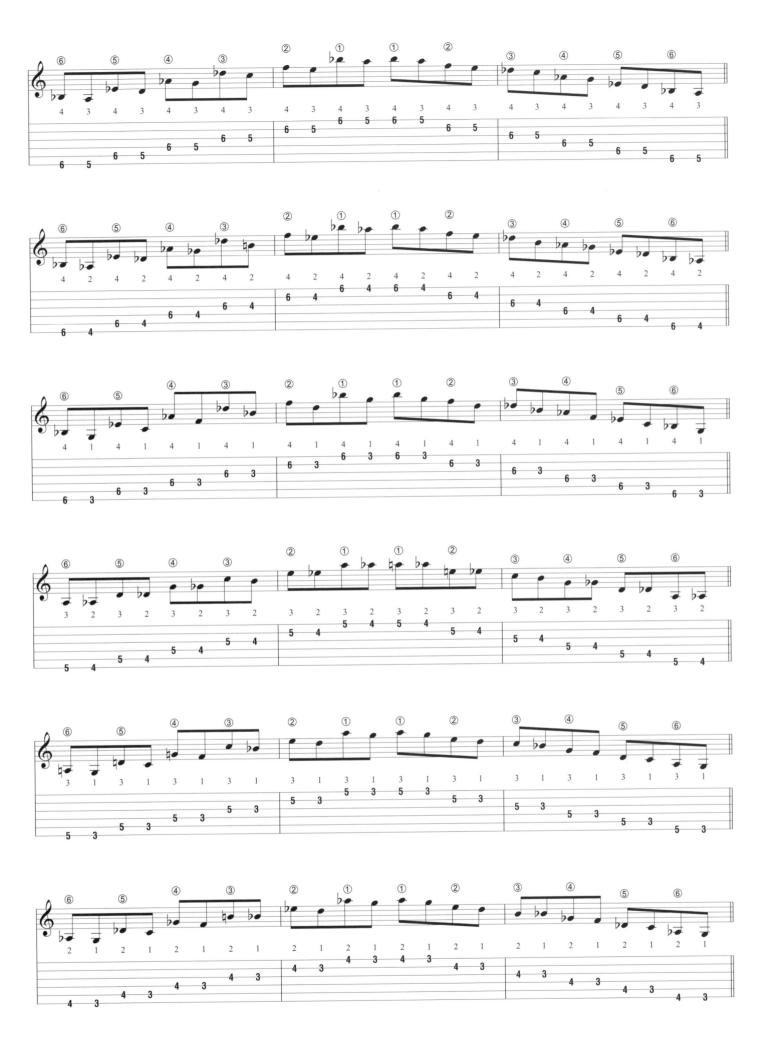

Practice these examples slowly at first, picking each note using strict alternate picking, building speed gradually. After gaining some facility with them, they should be practiced with slur phrasing as per the following examples.

Example 1

Example 2

For a slur going up between the two notes, pick the first note only and fret the second note by heavily dropping down the indicated finger. This is also known as a *hammer-on*.

To perform a slur going downward between two notes, put both fretting fingers in place, pick the first note, then pull off that fretting finger with a slight downward snap, sounding the second note. This is also known as a *pull-off*.

EXAMPLES OF SLUR EXERCISES

Use the same fingerings as the coinciding examples on the previous pages.

Ex. 269

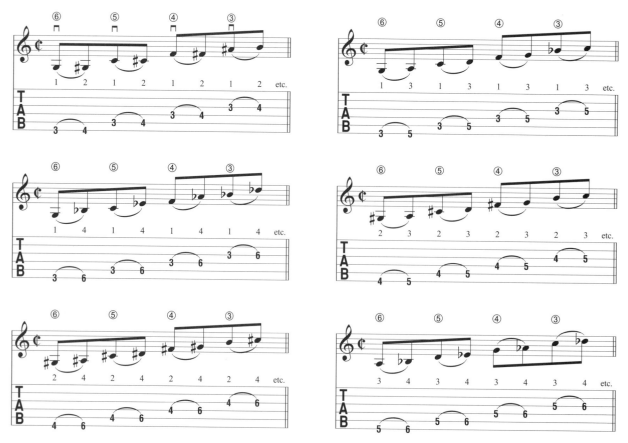

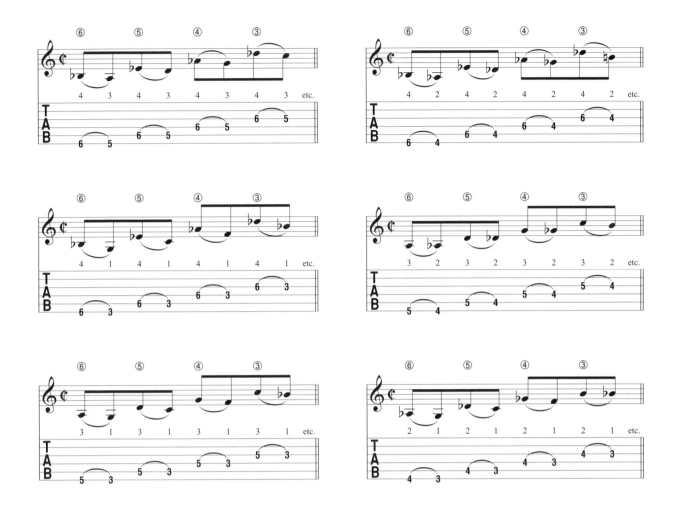

SLIDES

The following examples incorporate another slur technique: the *slide*. A slide is notated using a slur plus a diagonal line between the notes indicating the direction of the slide. To perform a slide, fret and pick the first note. Then, without lifting your finger, slide up or down to the next indicated note.

Ex. 270

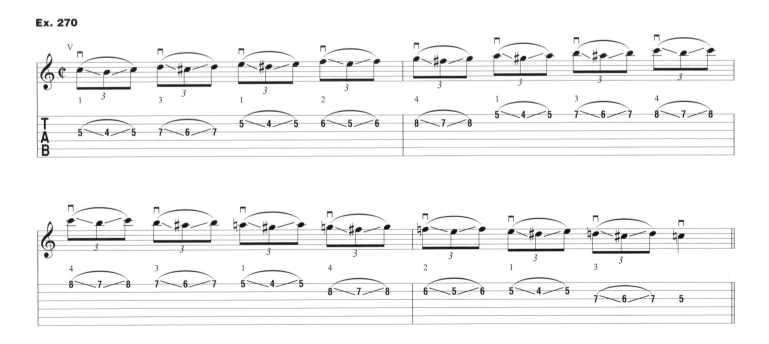

Ex. 271

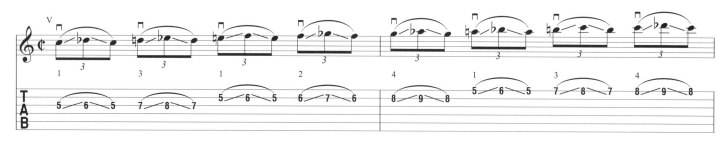

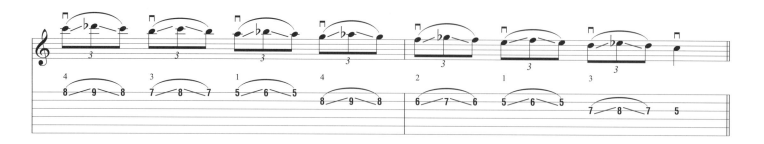

Ex. 272

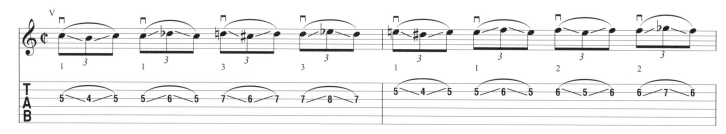

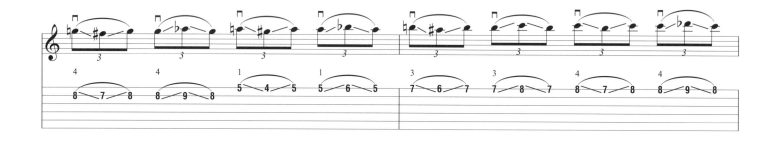

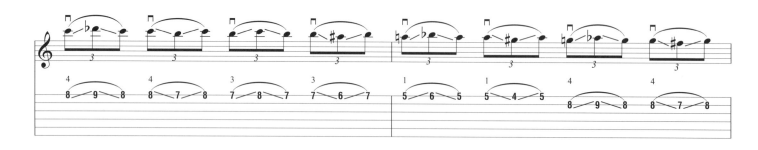

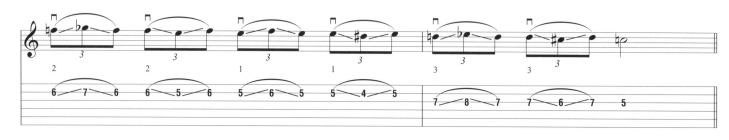

The following examples combine hammer-ons, pull-offs, and slides. Follow the fingerings and picking instructions for each triplet phrase.

Ex. 273

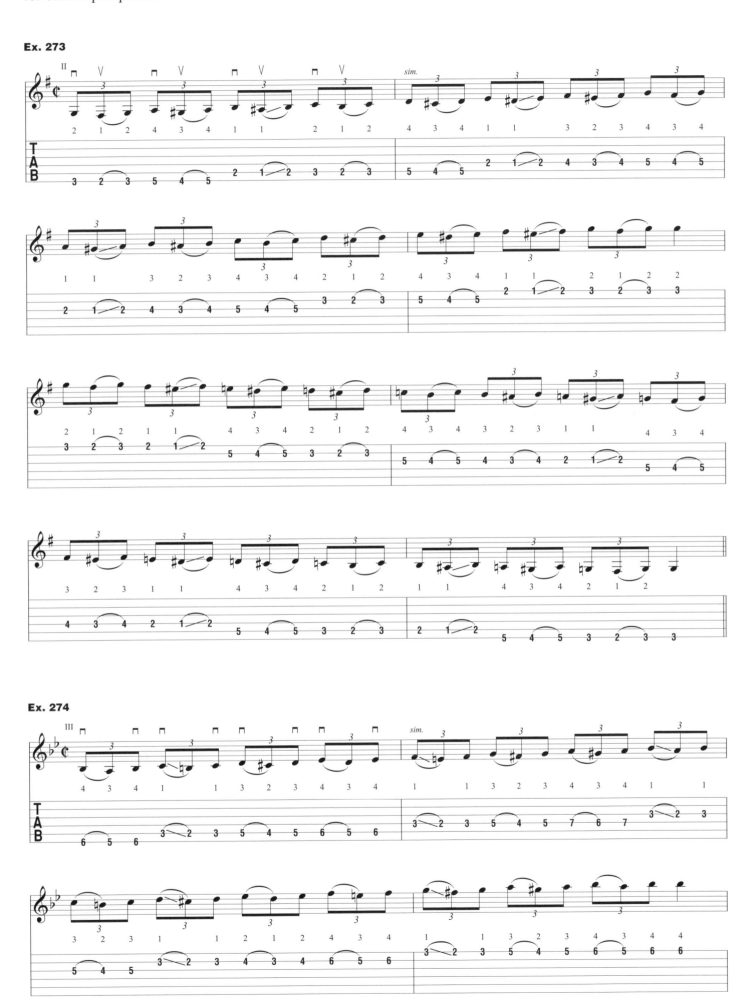

Ex. 274

139

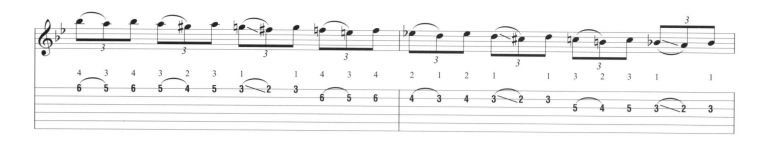

Ex. 275

SLURRED SCALES

Here are some examples of how to incorporate the slurs while playing the C major scale. Different positions and phrasings are featured. These can also be done in two octave scales and in many more positions than are shown here. They should be practiced in all keys.

Ex. 276

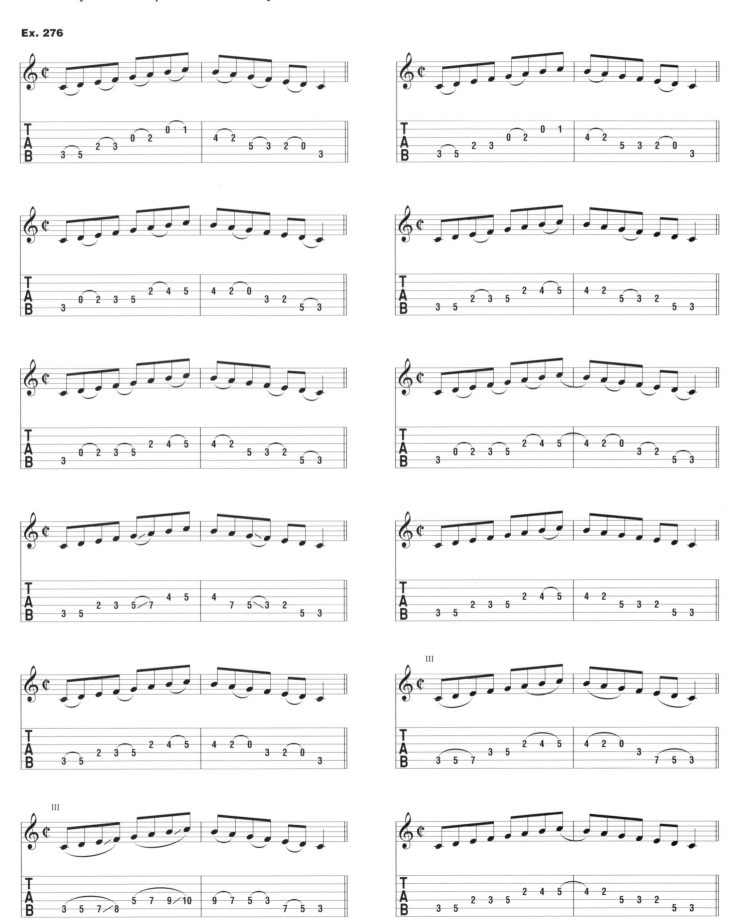

Practice the following pattern on all adjacent strings. Play very slowly at first, making sure each note sounds full.

Ex. 277

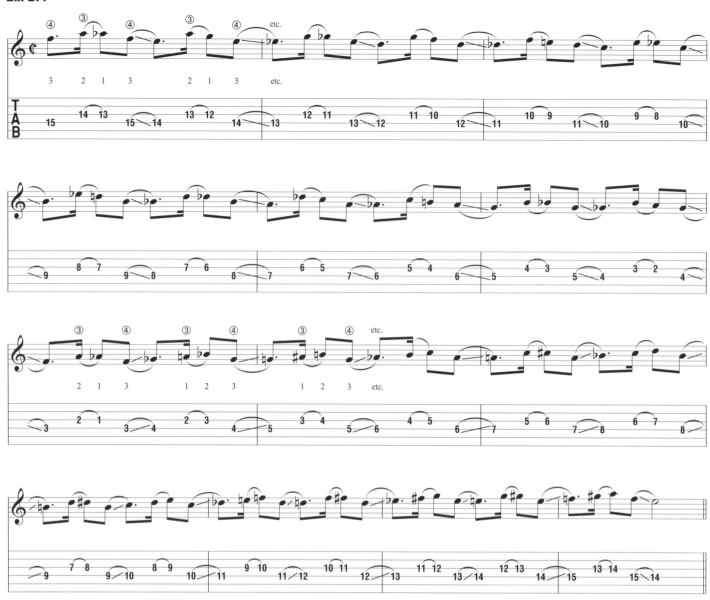

Practice the above example using the following four alternate fingerings.

Ex. 278

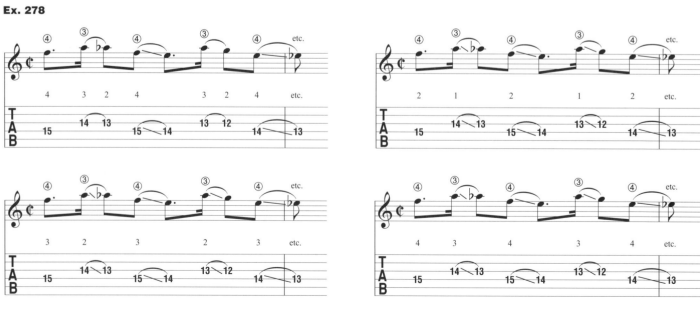

ARPEGGIOS

ARPEGGIO PICKING

Practice the following arpeggio fingerings chromatically up the fretboard as far as you can go, using alternate picking throughout.

Numbers in circles (①) denote strings.

Numbers plain (2) denote fingering.

Practice slowly to gain accuracy first. Once you've achieved this, speed will come naturally.

Ex. 279

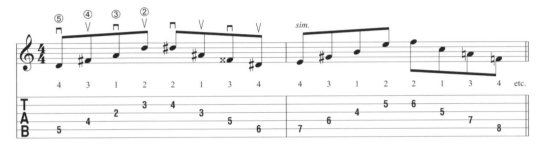

Ex. 280

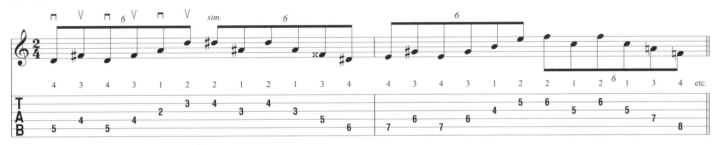

Ex. 281

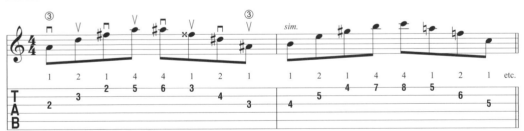

Ex. 282

Ex. 283

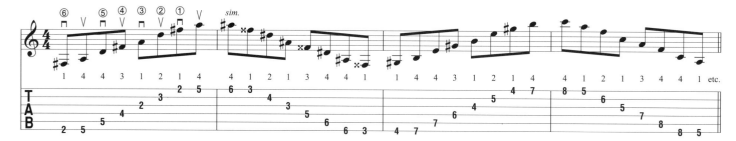

Ex. 284

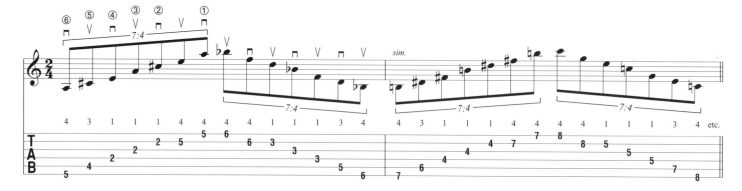

THE MAJOR CHORDS IN ARPEGGIO FORM

Major chords are built from the 1st, 3rd, and 5th tones of the major scale.

Ex. 285

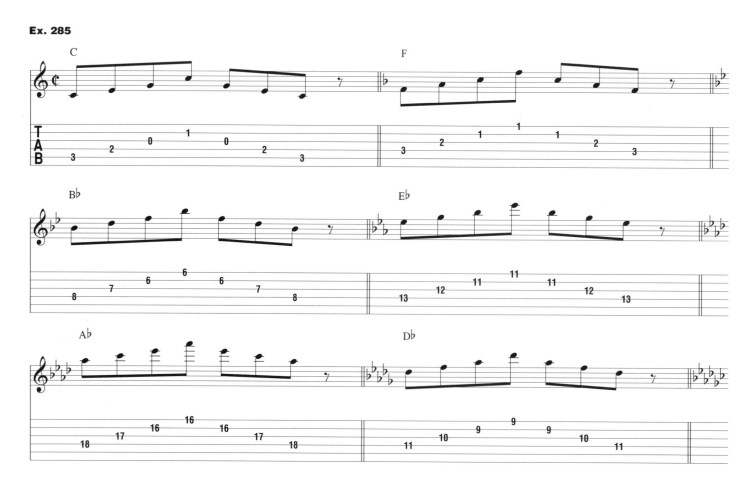

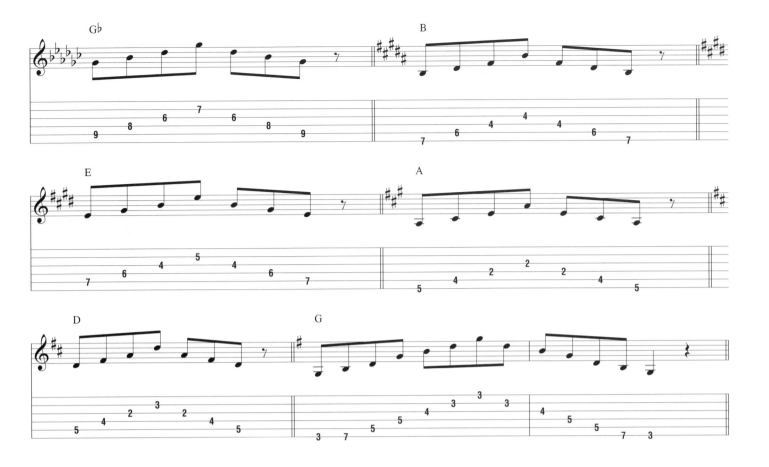

THE MINOR CHORDS IN ARPEGGIO FORM

Minor chords are built from the 1st, 3rd, and 5th tones of the minor scale.

Ex. 286

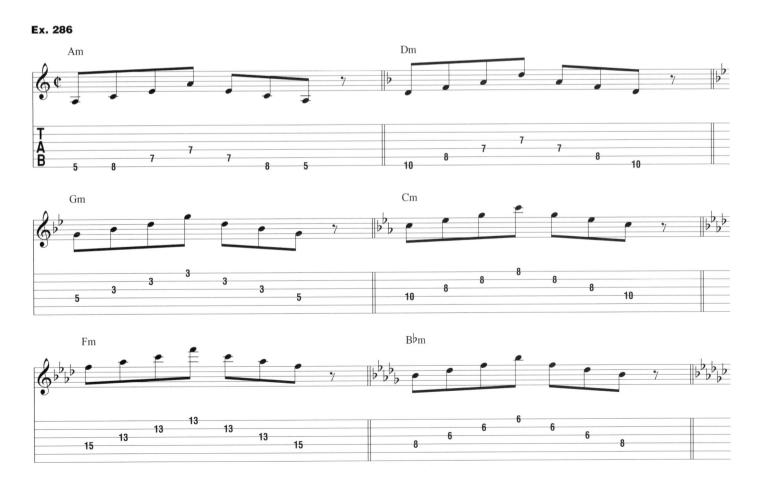

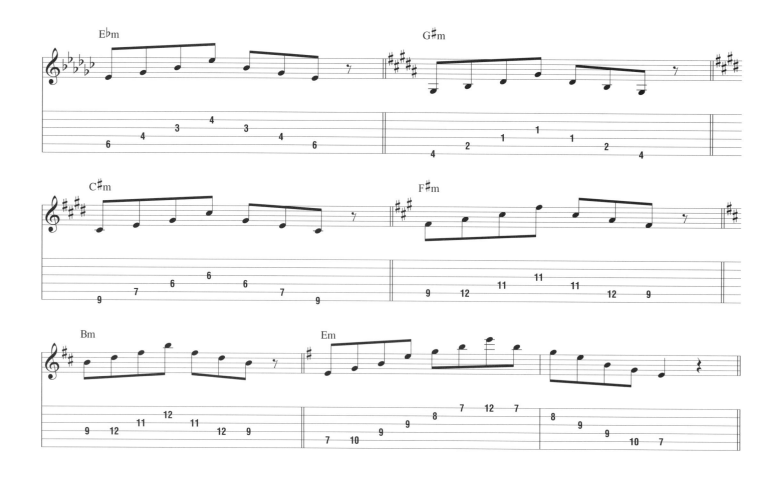

THE AUGMENTED CHORDS IN ARPEGGIO FORM

Augmented chords are built from the 1st, 3rd, and #5th tones of the major scale.

Ex. 287

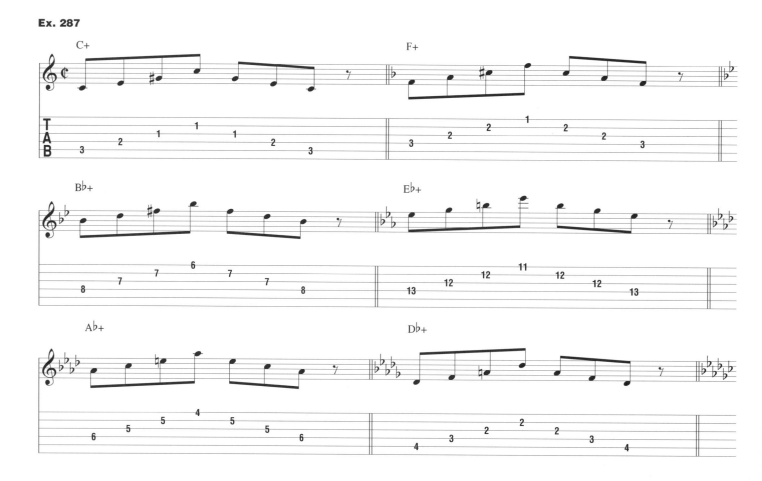

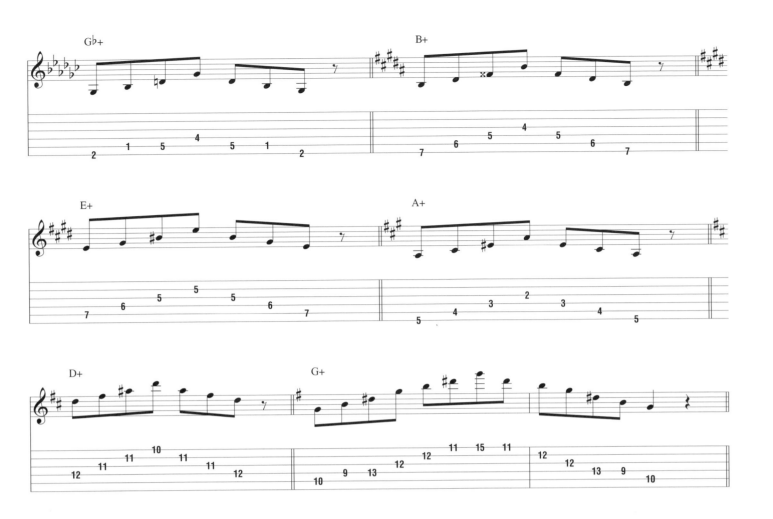

LONG FORM ARPEGGIOS

Ex. 288

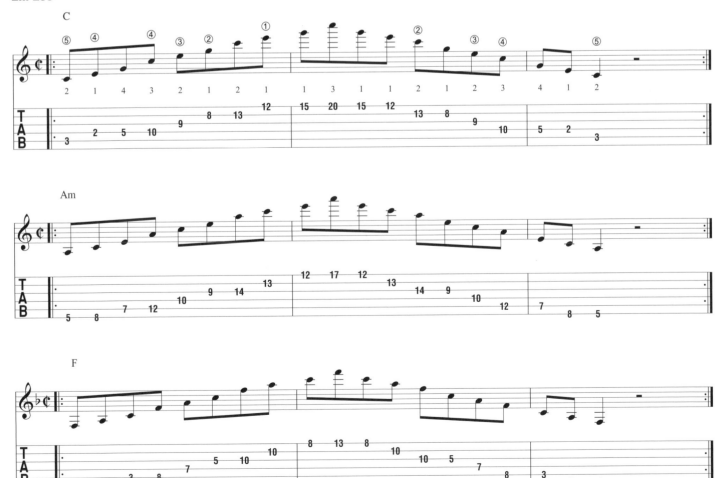

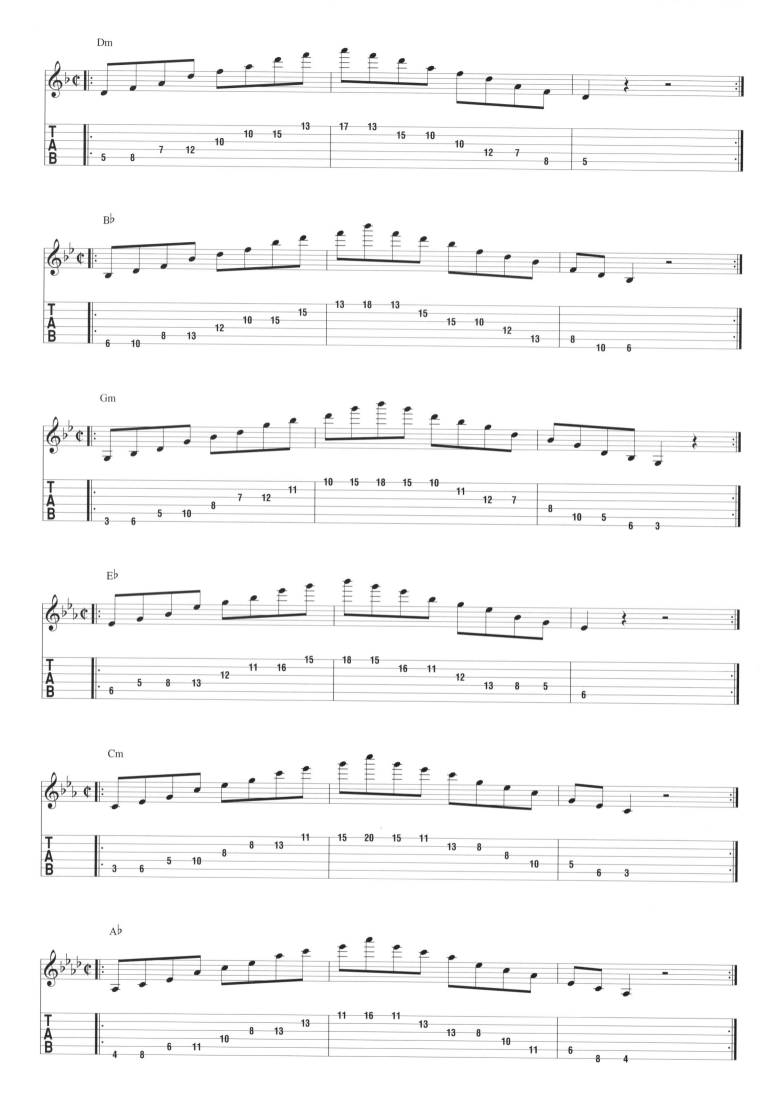

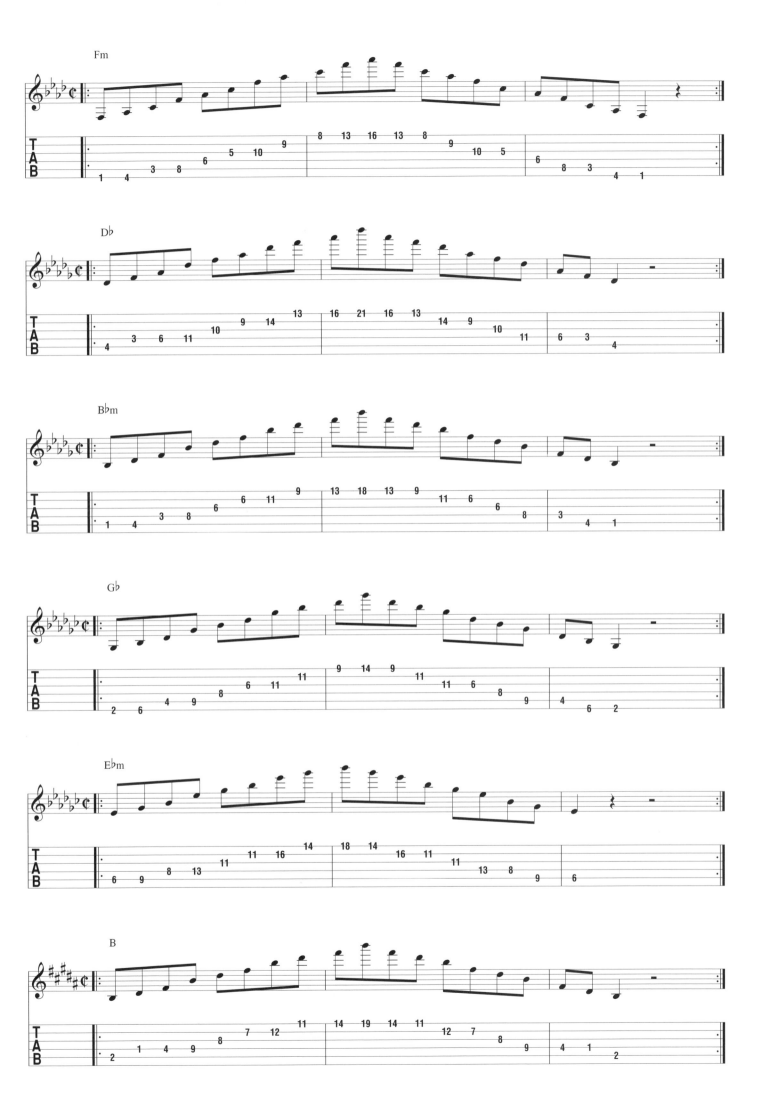

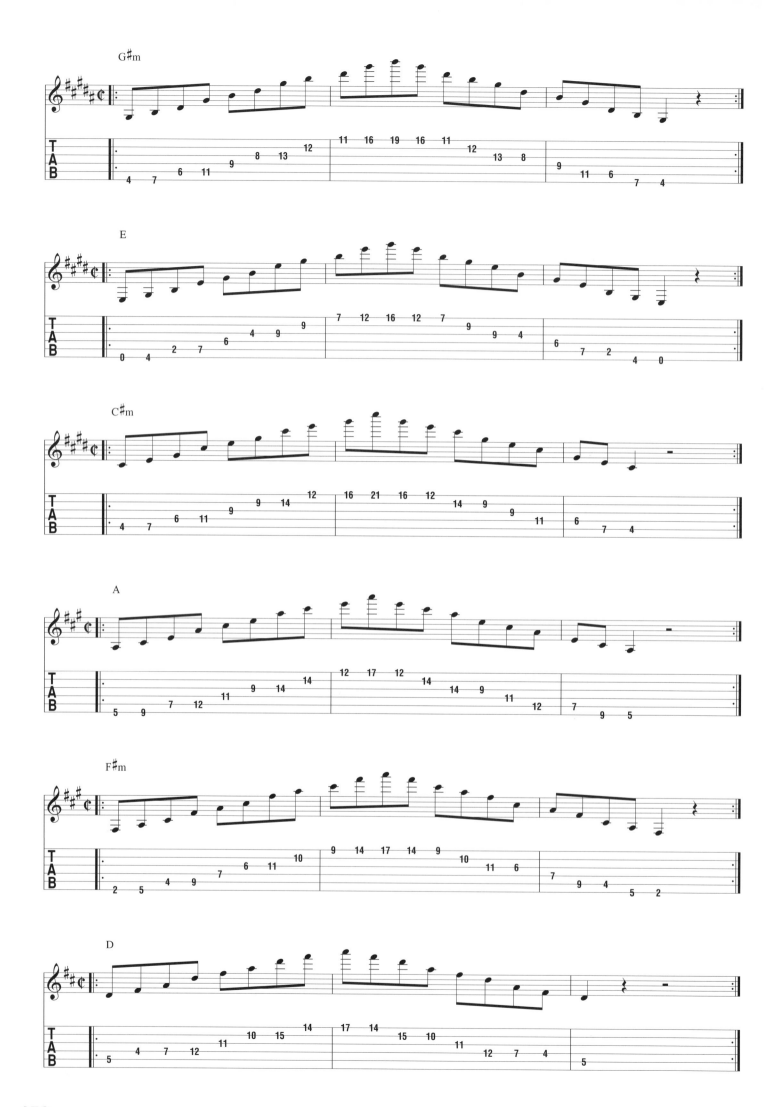

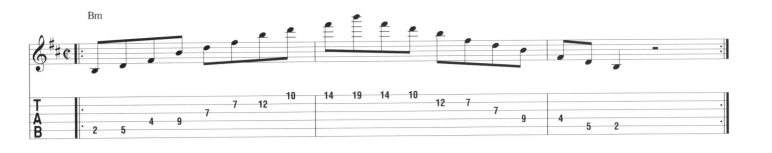

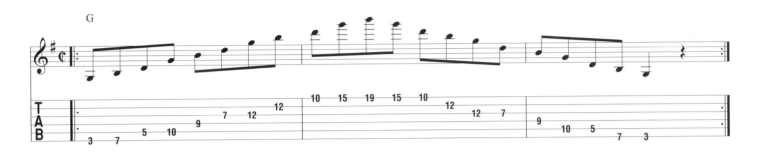

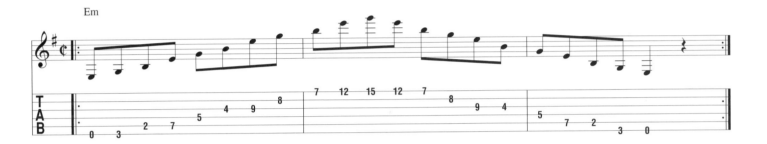

OCTAVES

Mute the string between the root note and octave by lightly touching the string with another finger, or by slightly straightening your first finger and resting it against the string. Muted strings are indicated with an "x" in the tab. For an octave separated by two frets, fret the notes with your first and third fingers; for an octave separated by three frets, fret the notes with your first and fourth fingers.

Ex. 289

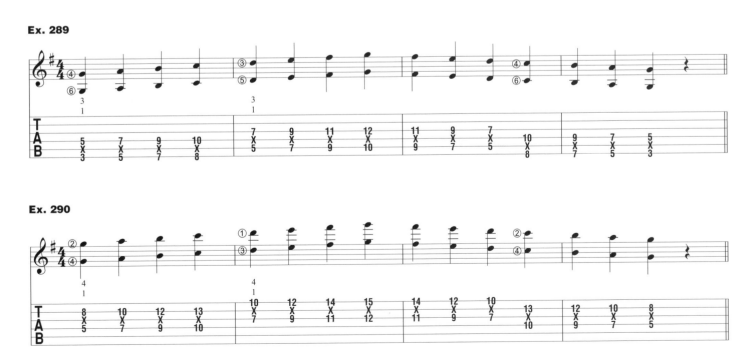

Ex. 290

Use the previous fingerings to play the following exercise. Practice using all downstrokes first. Then try alternate picking throughout. Transpose the exercise and play it in all keys.

Ex. 291

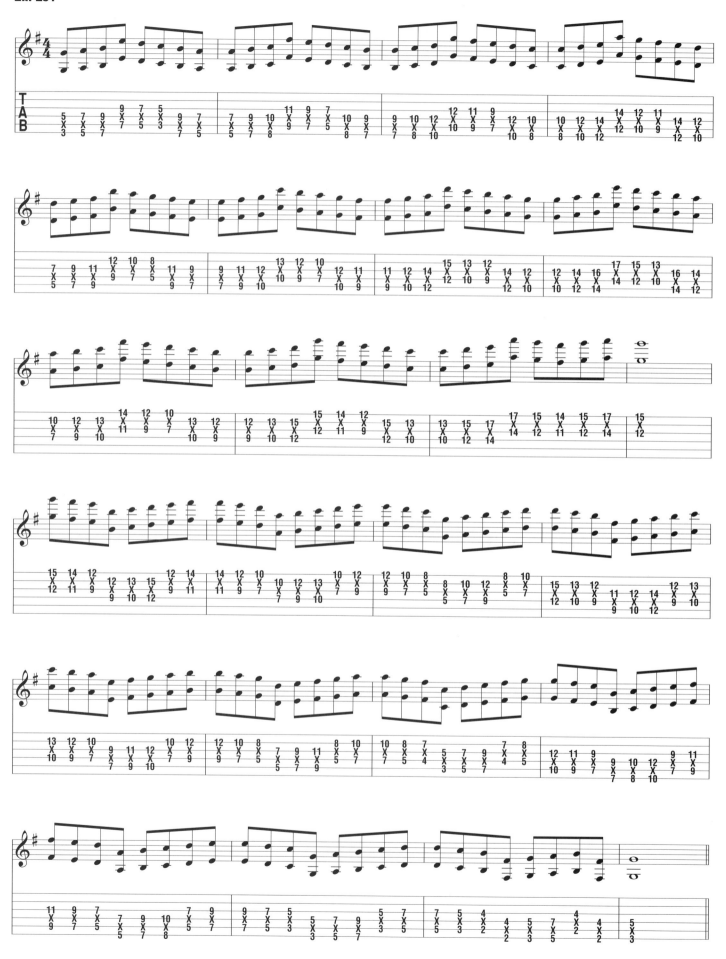

DIMINISHED SCALES
AND EXERCISES

Ex. 292

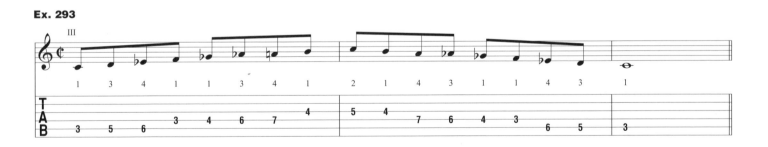

Here's an alternate fingering for the descending part of the above diminished scale.

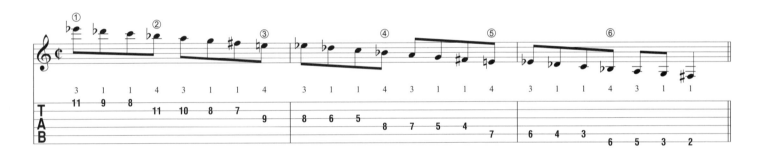

Ex. 293

Ex. 294

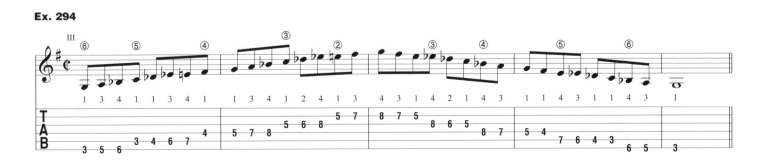

DIMINISHED SEVENTH CHORD EXERCISE

Diminished seventh chords are built from the 1st, ♭3rd, ♭5th, and ♭♭7th steps of the major scale. Practice the following exercise chromatically up the fretboard as far as possible.

Ex. 295

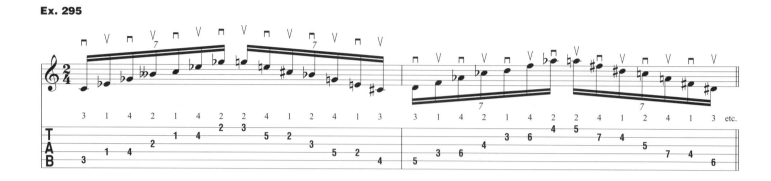

MAJOR SIXTH CHORDS

Major sixth chords are built from the 1st, 3rd, 5th, and 6th steps of the major scale.

Ex. 296

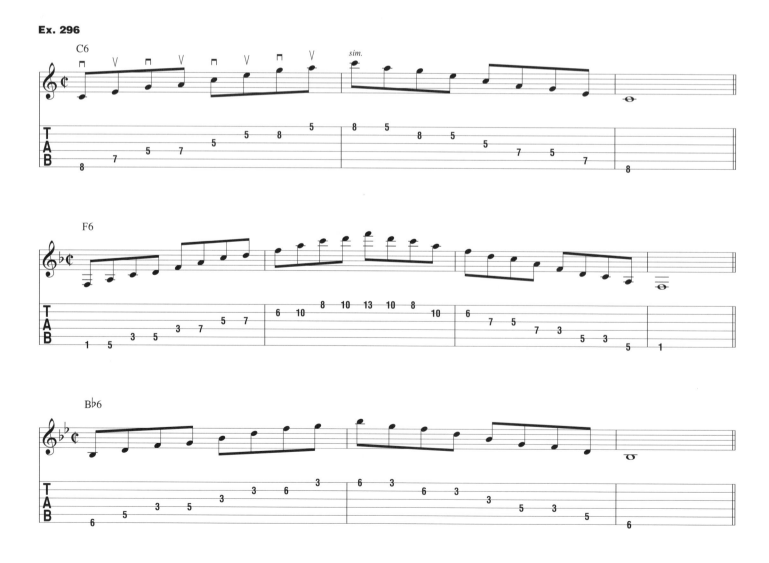

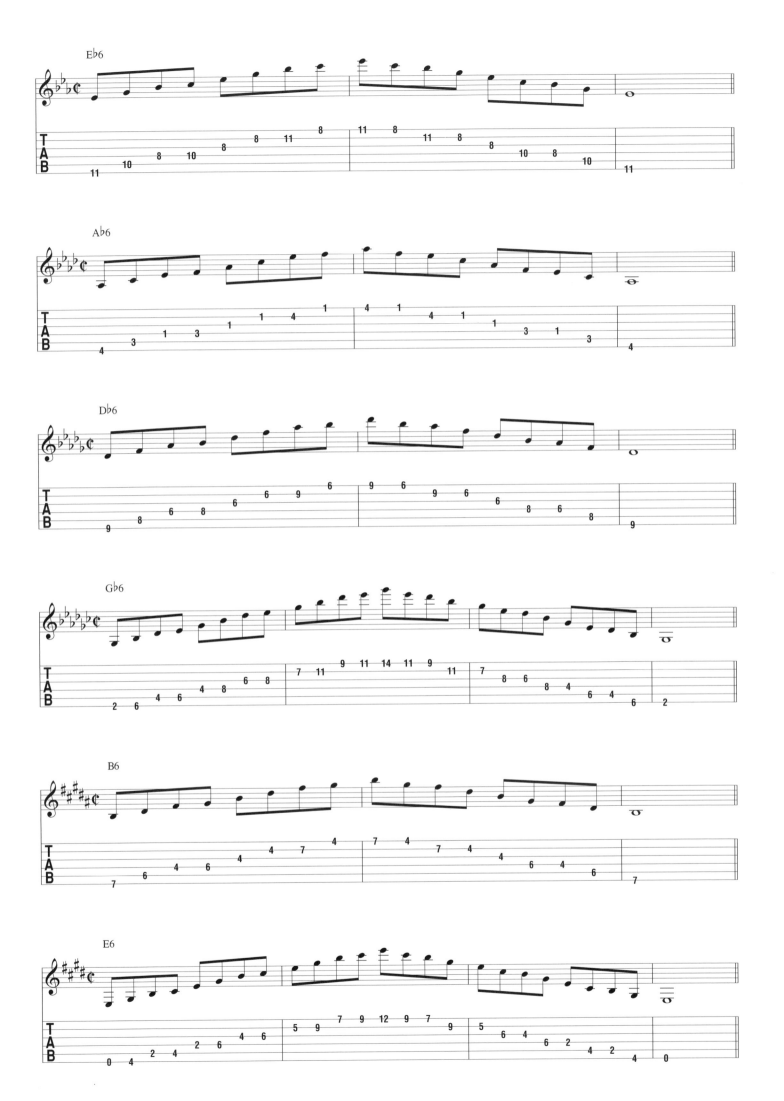

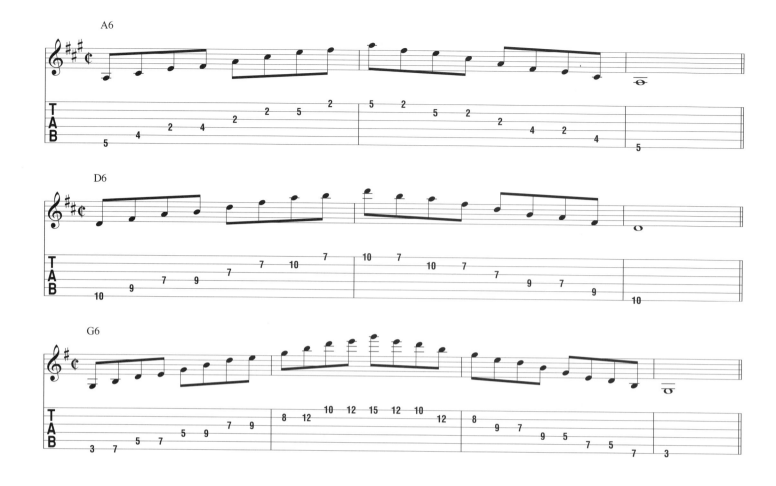

MAJOR SEVENTH CHORDS

Major seventh chords are built from the 1st, 3rd, 5th, and 7th steps of the major scale.

Ex. 297

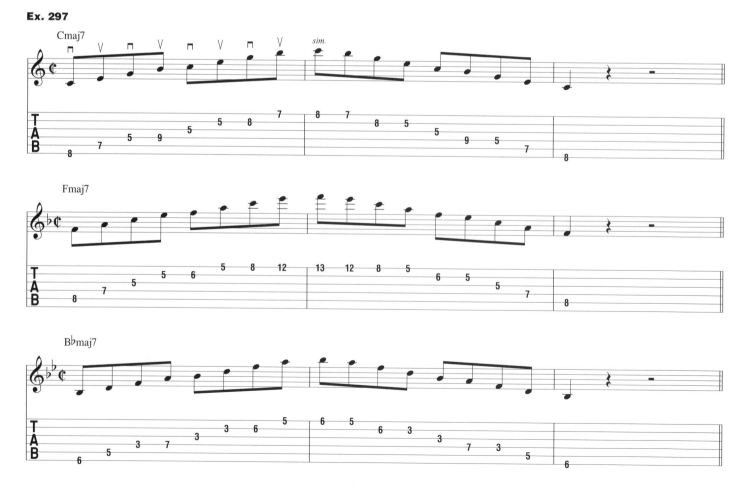

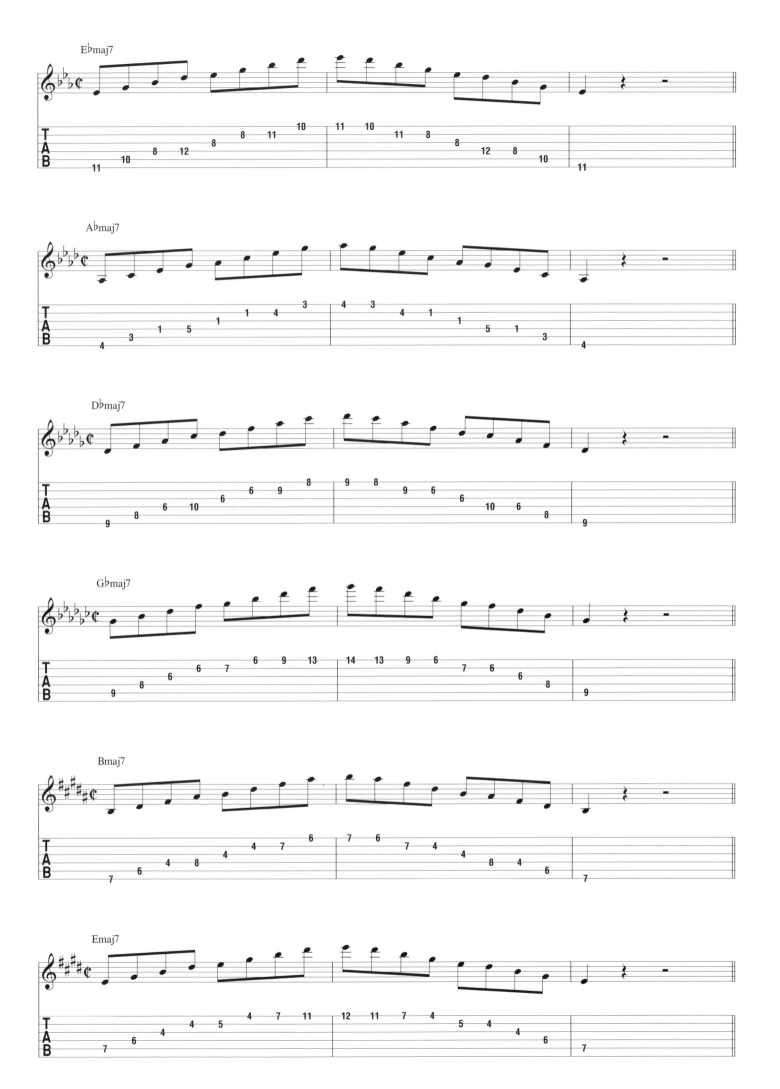

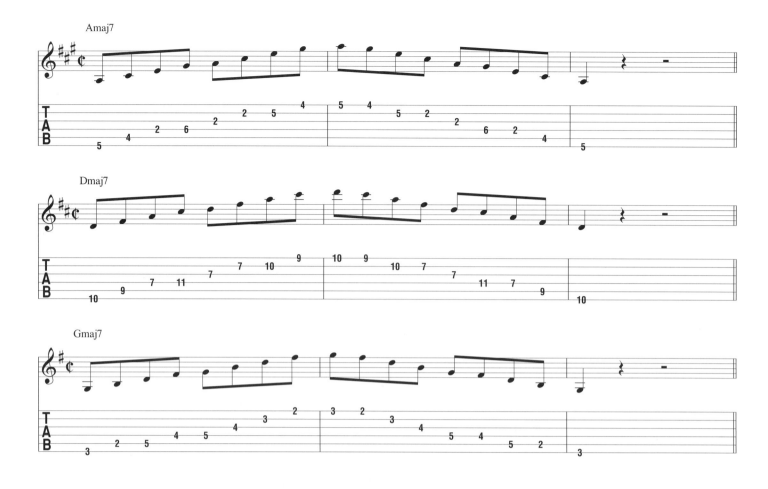

DOMINANT SEVENTH SCALES

Lower the 7th tone of the major scale by a half step (one fret). Play the scale in all keys using the same variations as with the major scale.

Ex. 298

Ex. 299

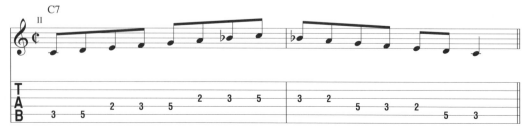

Ex. 300

DOMINANT SEVENTH CHORD EXERCISES

Dominant seventh chords are built from the 1st, 3rd, 5th, and ♭7th steps of the major scale.

Ex. 301

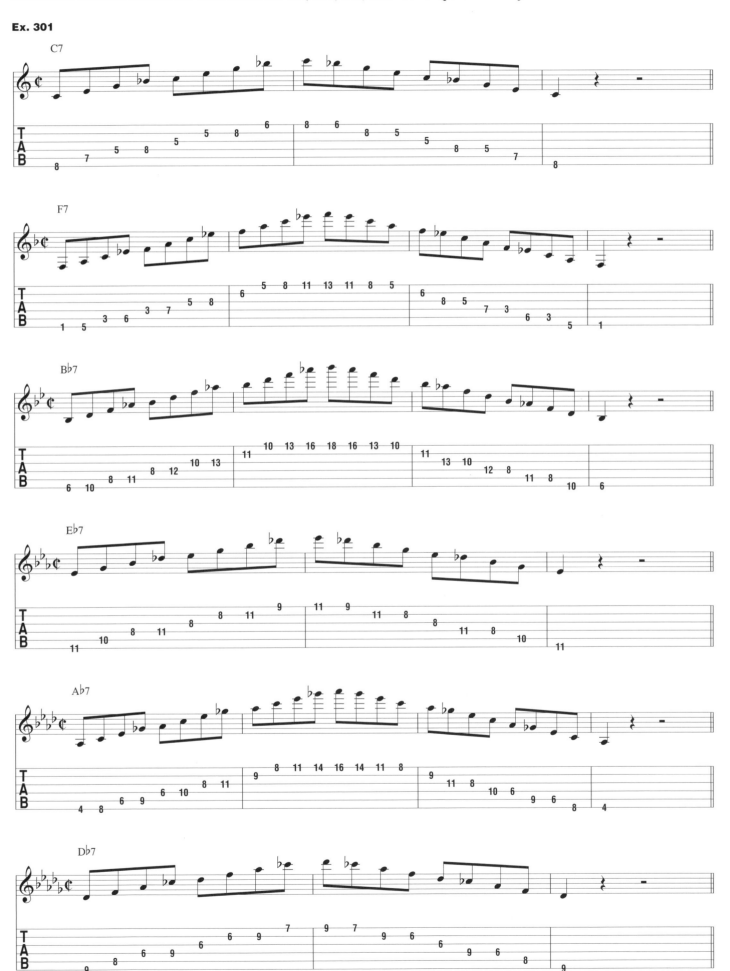

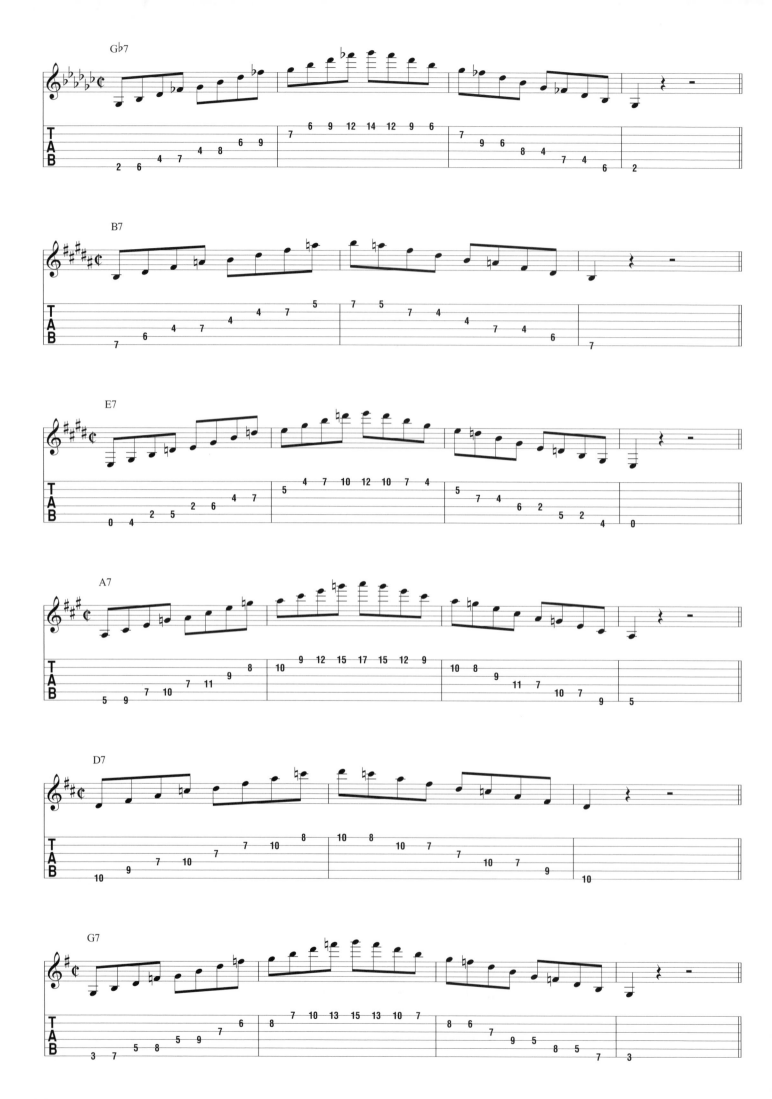

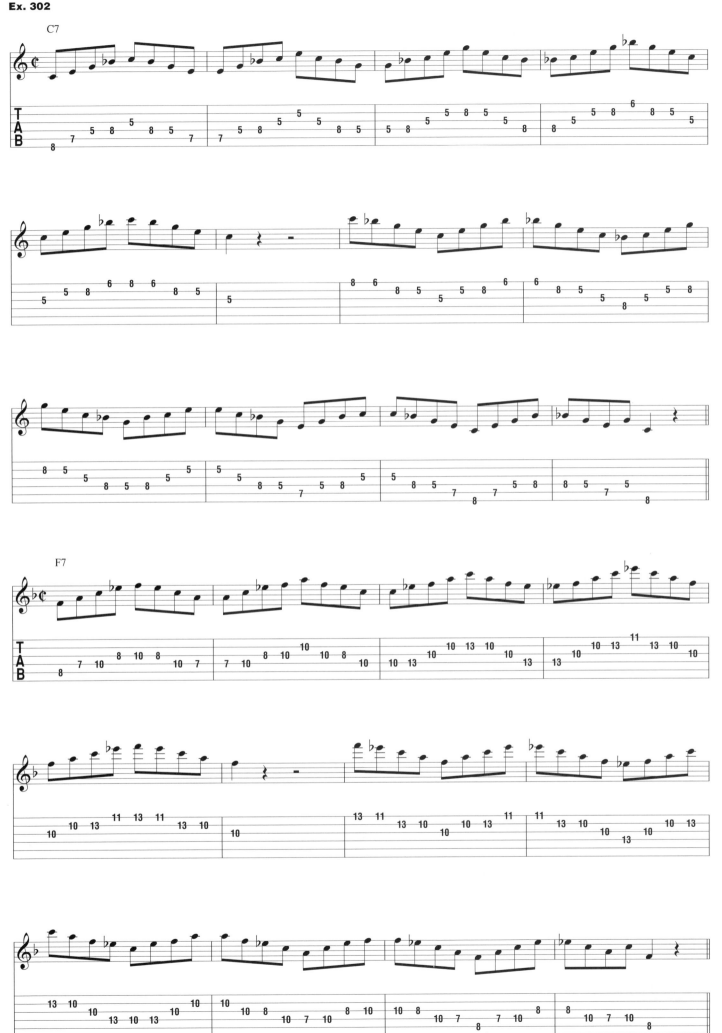

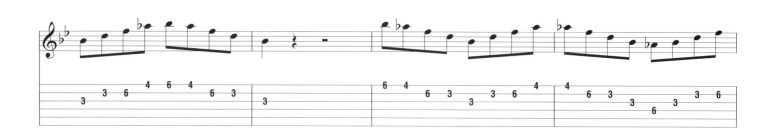

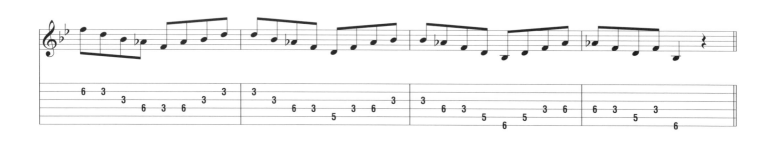

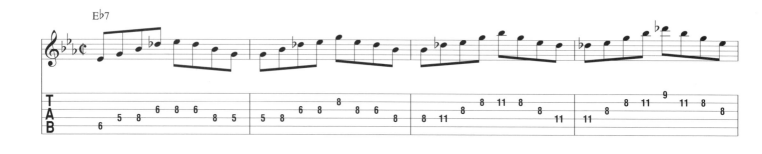

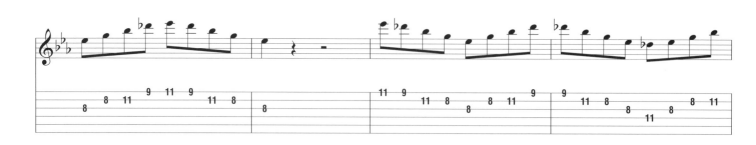

162

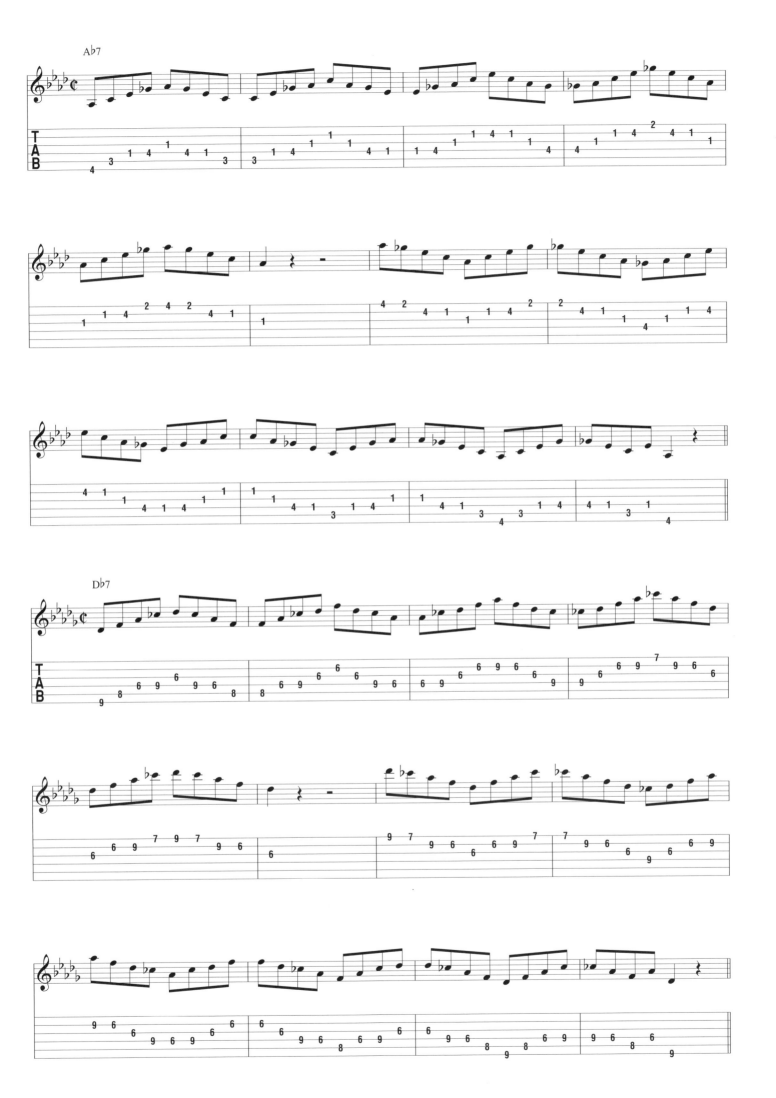

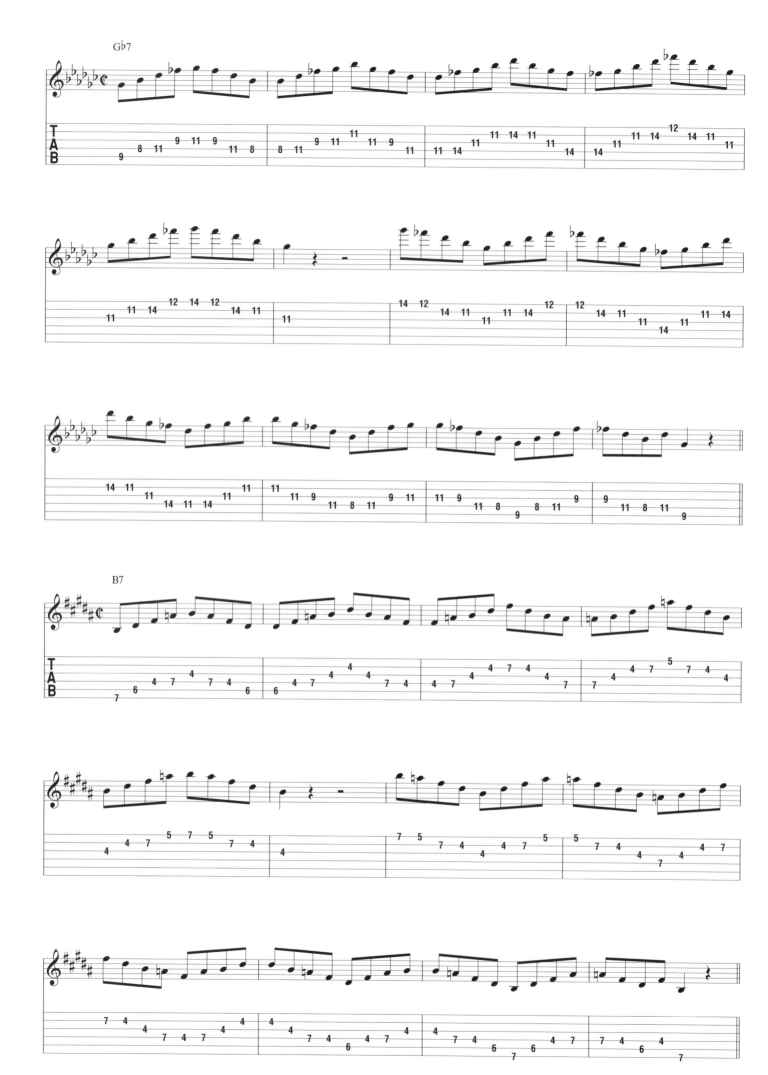

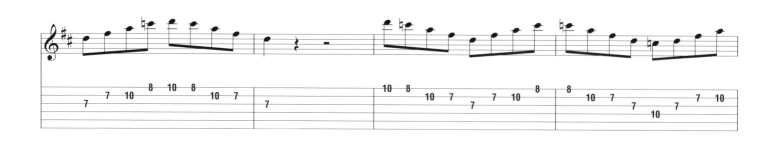

G7

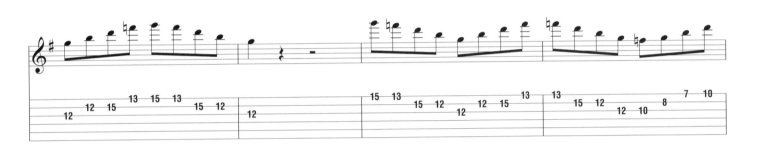

Here's an exercise for going from dominant seventh to dominant seventh in the circle of fifths.

Ex. 303

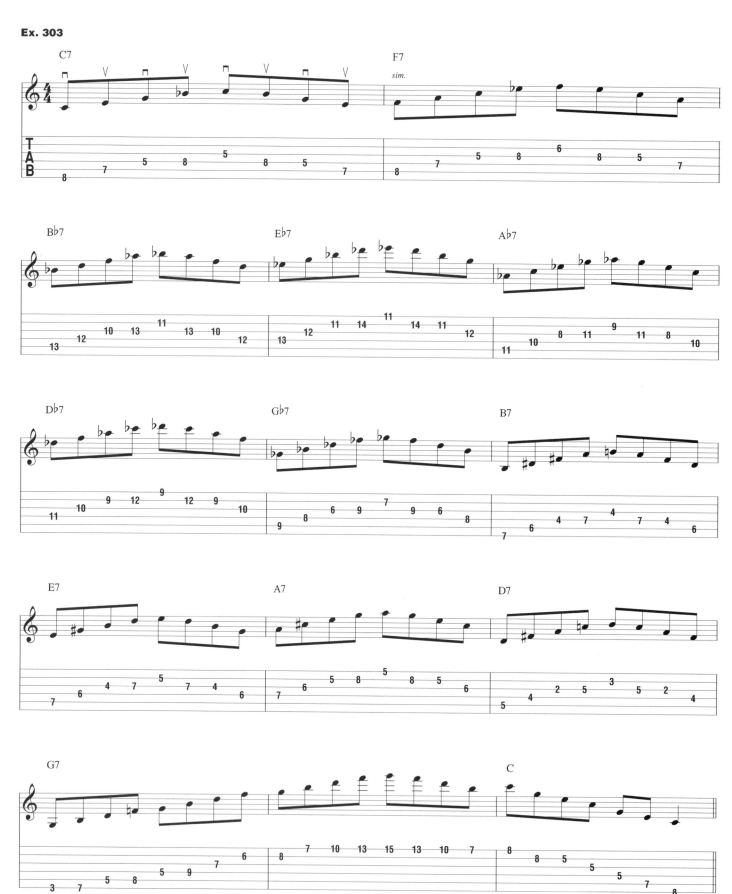

RESOLVING SEVENTH CHORDS

Ex. 304

Here's a progression exercise for going from major to dominant seventh to major in the circle of fifths.

Ex. 305

171

MINOR SEVENTH SCALES

Lower the 3rd and 7th tones of the major scale by a half step (one fret). Play the scale in all keys.

Ex. 306

MINOR SEVENTH CHORD EXERCISES

Minor seventh chords are built from the 1st, ♭3rd, 5th, and ♭7th steps of the major scale.

Ex. 307

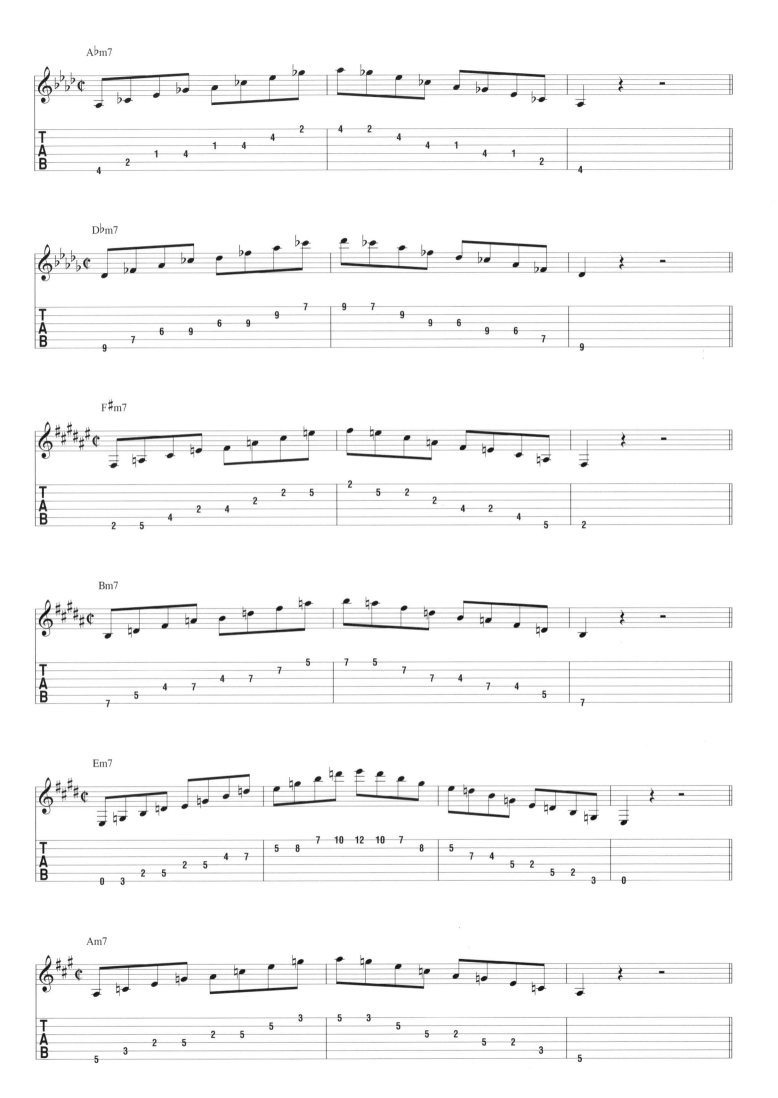

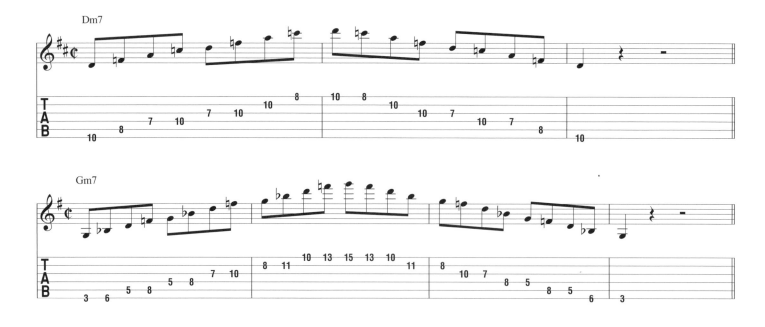

Here's a minor seventh inversions exercise. Use the following patterns with the other minor seventh chords as well.

Ex. 308

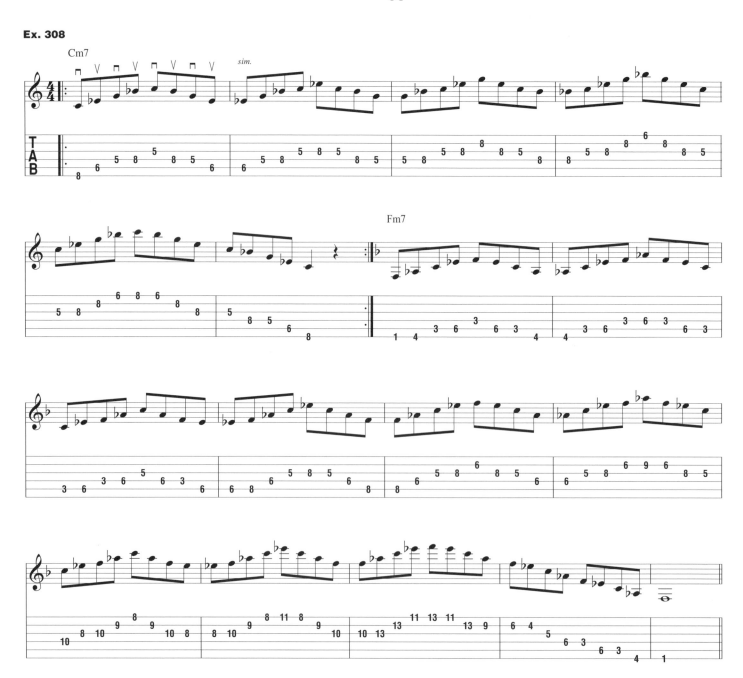

MINOR SEVENTH TO DOMINANT SEVENTH

Ex. 309

176

Here's a progression exercise that combines the different arpeggios in each key.

Ex. 310

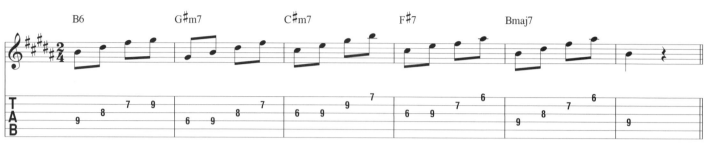

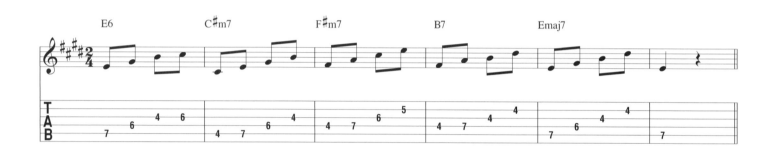

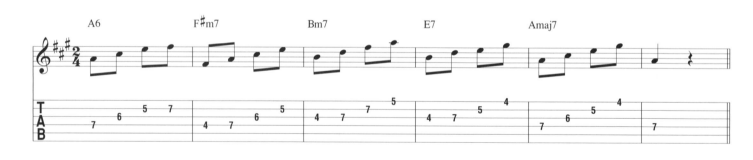

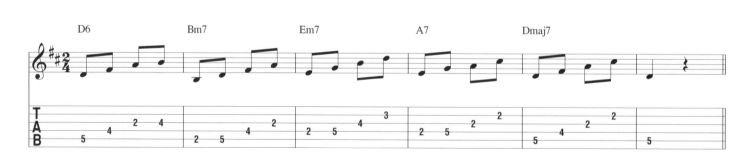

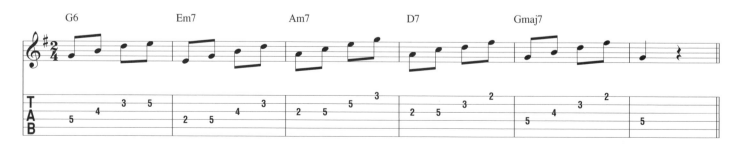

MINOR SEVENTH EXERCISE

Rake the pick across the strings in an even, unbroken motion as indicated by the picking symbols. Practice each figure chromatically up the fretboard.

Ex. 311

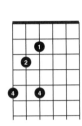
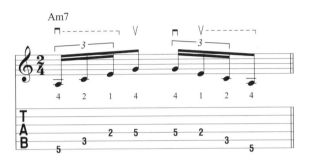

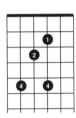
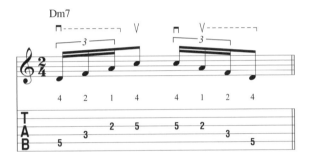

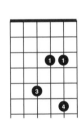
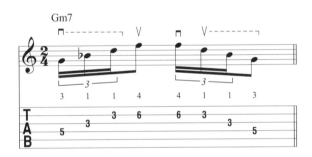

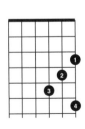
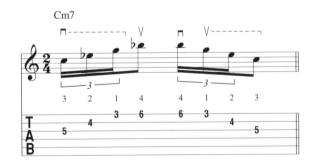

ALTERED DOMINANTS AND MINOR SEVENTHS

Transpose all of the scales and chords in this section to all keys and play them using the pattern variations from previous chapters.

MINOR SEVENTH FLATTED FIFTH SCALE

Lower the 3rd, 5th, and 7th steps of the major scale by a half step.

Ex. 312

MINOR SEVENTH FLATTED FIFTH CHORD

The minor seventh flatted fifth chord is made up of the 1st, ♭3rd, ♭5th, and ♭7th of any major scale and is used to resolve to dominant 7th chords.

Ex. 313

DOMINANT SEVENTH FLATTED FIFTH SCALE

Lower the 5th and 7th steps of the major scale by a half step.

Ex. 314

FLATTED FIFTH CHORD

The flatted fifth chord is made up of the 1st, 3rd, ♭5th, and ♭7th of any major scale and is used as an extension and a substitute for a dominant 7th chord.

Ex. 315

FLATTED FIFTH CHORD INVERSION

Ex. 316

Play in all keys.

CHORD PROGRESSION

Continue the following exercise by playing it in all keys.

Ex. 317

AUGMENTED SEVENTH CHORD

The augmented seventh chord is made up of the 1st, 3rd, #5th, and ♭7th of any major scale.

Ex. 318

AUGMENTED SEVENTH CHORD INVERSION

Ex. 319

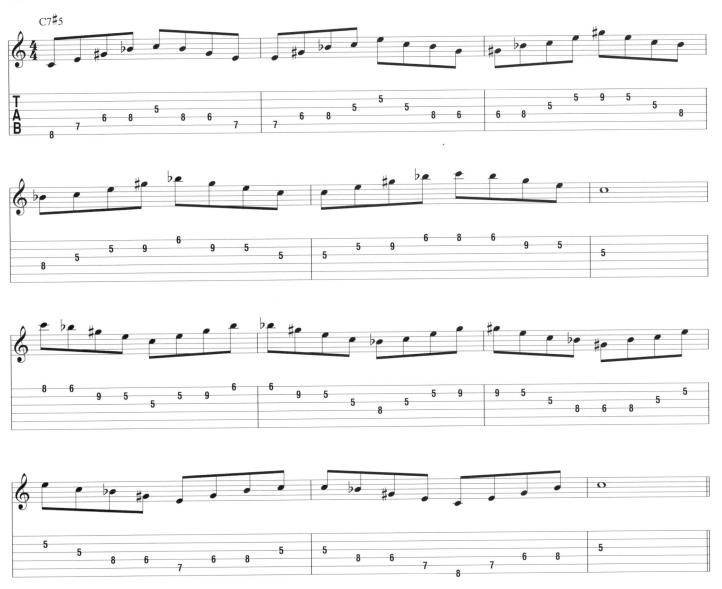

DOMINANT NINTH CHORD

The dominant ninth chord is made up of the 1st, 3rd, 5th, ♭7th, and 9th of any major scale and is used as an extension and a substitute for a dominant 7th chord.

Ex. 320

DOMINANT NINTH CHORD INVERSION

Ex. 321

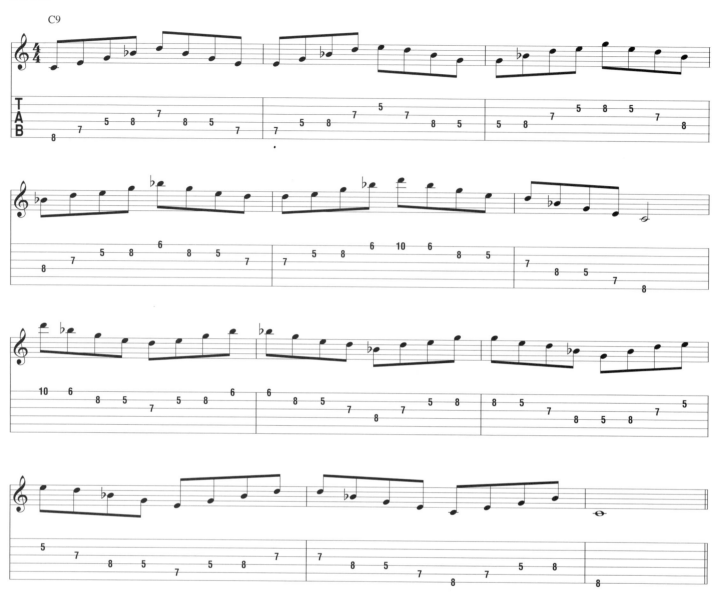

DOMINANT SEVENTH FLATTED NINTH SCALE

Ex. 322

DOMINANT SEVENTH FLATTED NINTH CHORD

The dominant seventh flatted ninth chord is made up of the 1st, 3rd, 5th, ♭7th, and ♭9th of any major scale and is used as an extension and a substitute for a dominant 7th chord.

Ex. 323

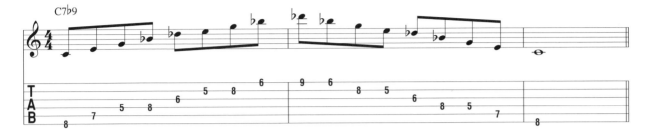

DOMINANT SEVENTH AUGMENTED NINTH CHORD

The dominant seventh augmented ninth chord is made up of the 1st, 3rd, 5th, ♭7th, and ♯9th of any major scale and is used as an extension and a substitute for a dominant 9th chord.

Ex. 324

DOMINANT ELEVENTH CHORD

The dominant eleventh chord is made up of the 1st, 3rd, 5th, ♭7th, 9th, and 11th of any major scale and is used as an extension and a substitute for a dominant 9th chord.

Ex. 325

AUGMENTED ELEVENTH CHORD

The augmented eleventh chord is made up of the 1st, 3rd, 5th, ♭7th, 9th, and ♯11th of any major scale and is used as an extension and a substitute for a dominant 9th chord.

Ex. 326

AUGMENTED ELEVENTH SCALES

Ex. 327

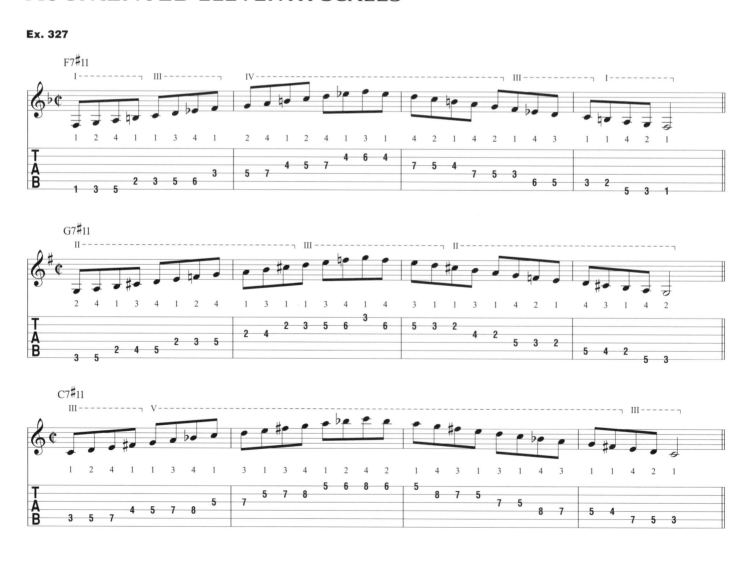

Ex. 328

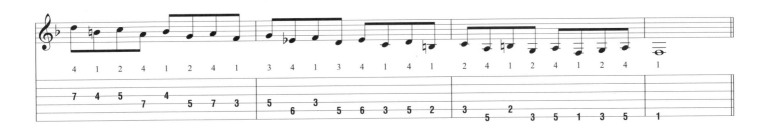

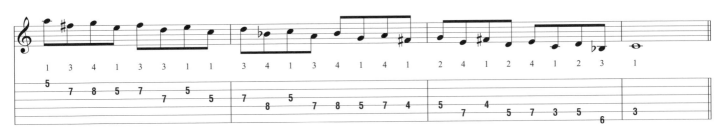

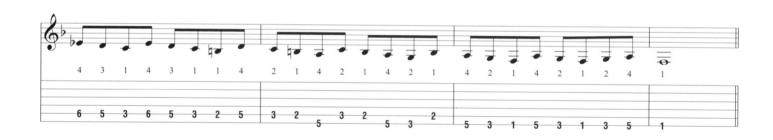

C7#11

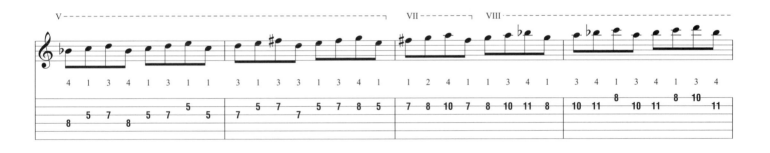

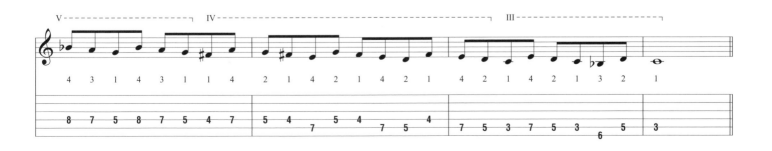

THIRTEENTH CHORD

The thirteenth chord is made up of the 1st, 3rd, 5th, ♭7th, 9th, 11th, and 13th of any major scale and is used as an extension and a substitution for a dominant 7th and 9th chord.

Ex. 329

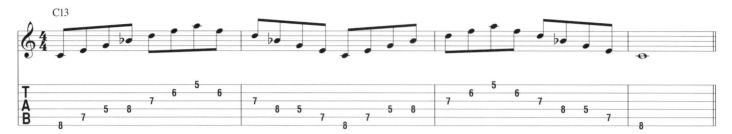

THIRTEENTH FLAT NINTH CHORD

The thirteenth flat ninth chord is made up of the 1st, 3rd, 5th, ♭7th, ♭9th, 11th, and 13th of any major scale and is used as an extension and a substitution for a dominant 7th and ♭9th chord.

Ex. 330

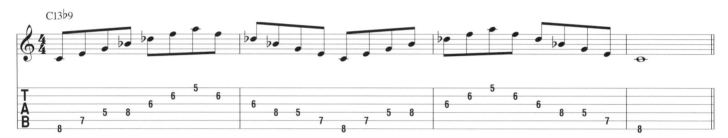

PROGRESSION EXERCISE

Practice the following exercise chromatically up the fretboard. After mastering it in 4/4 time, practice it in 6/8 time as well.

Ex. 331

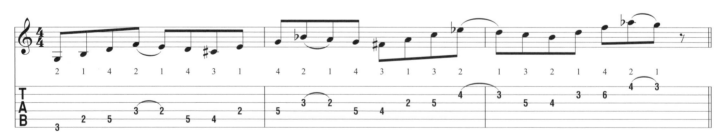

Ex. 332

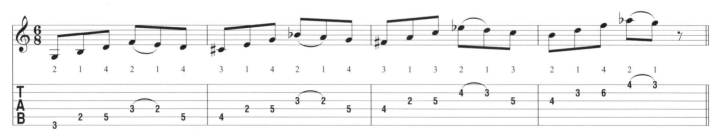

RIGHT HAND EXERCISES AND KEYBOARD HARMONY

MAJOR SCALES IN 3RDS

Practice the following exercise in different octaves. First play through it using all downstrokes; then play it using alternate picking.

Ex. 333

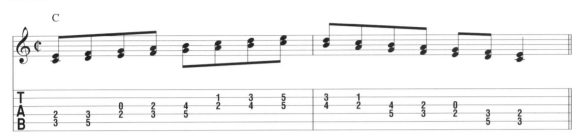

HARMONIC MINOR SCALES IN 3RDS

Practice the following exercise in different octaves. First play through it using all downstrokes; then play it using alternate picking.

Ex. 334

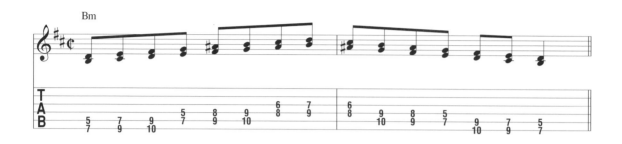

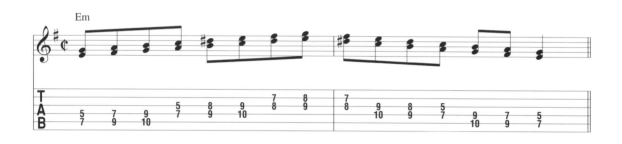

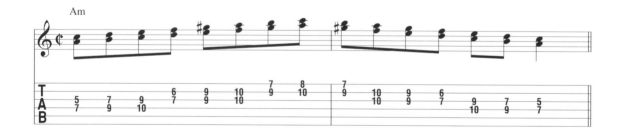

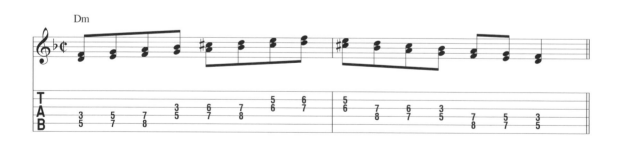

194

MELODIC MINOR SCALES IN 3RDS

Practice the following exercise in different octaves. First play through it using all downstrokes; then play it using alternate picking.

Ex. 335

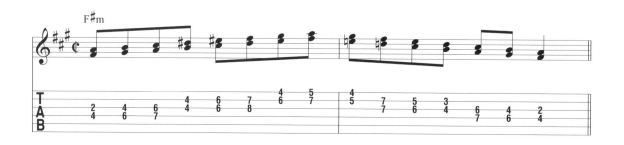

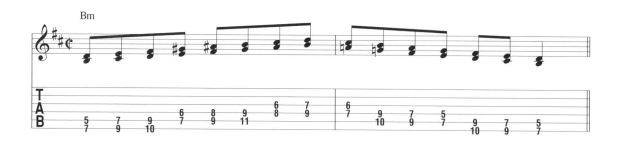

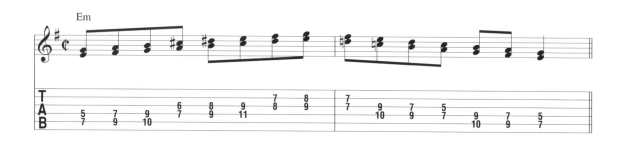

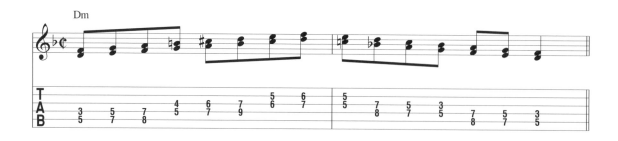

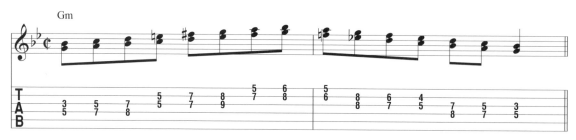

196

WHOLE TONE SCALES IN 3RDS

Ex. 336

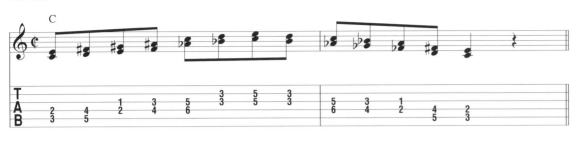

TRIADS

Ex. 337

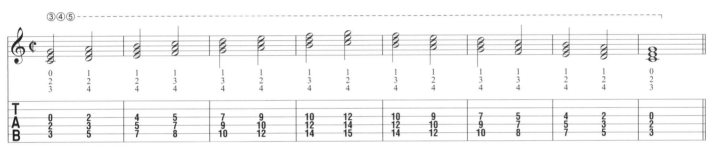

Practice these arpeggiated triads using consistent sweep picking as indicated by the picking symbols.

Ex. 338

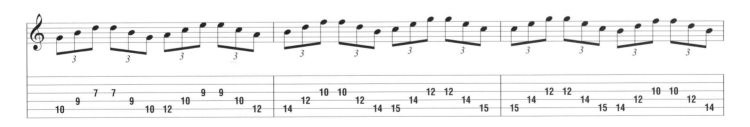

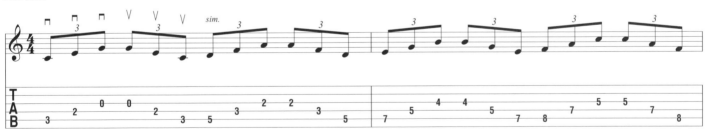

Practice each example as written in a half-note rhythm and then play each in an arpeggiated triplet rhythm as shown in the previous example.

Ex. 339

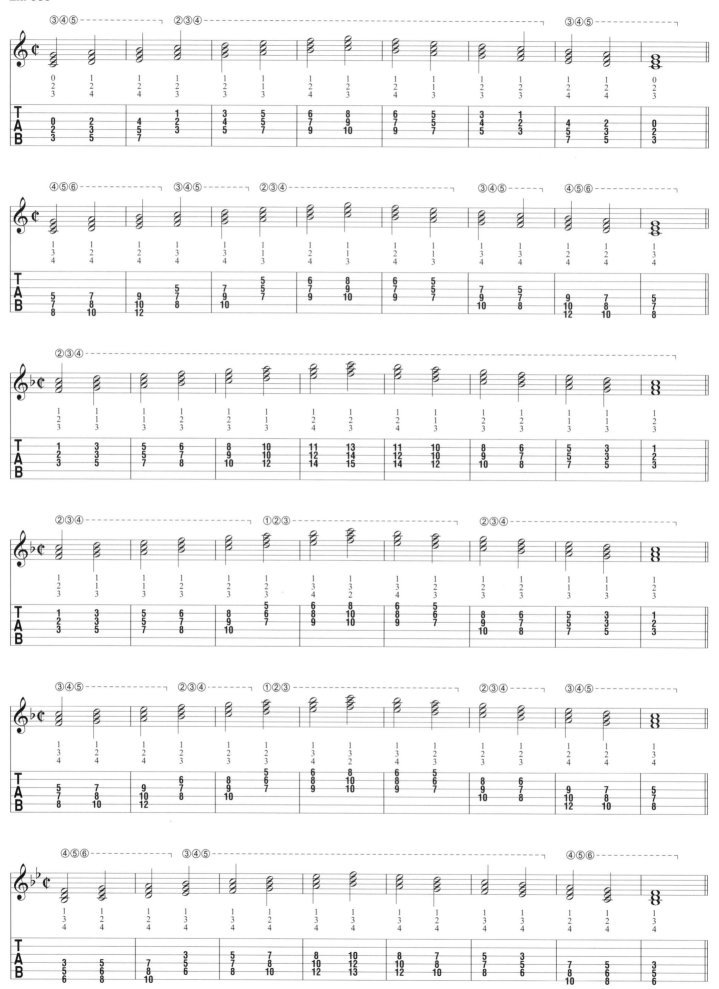

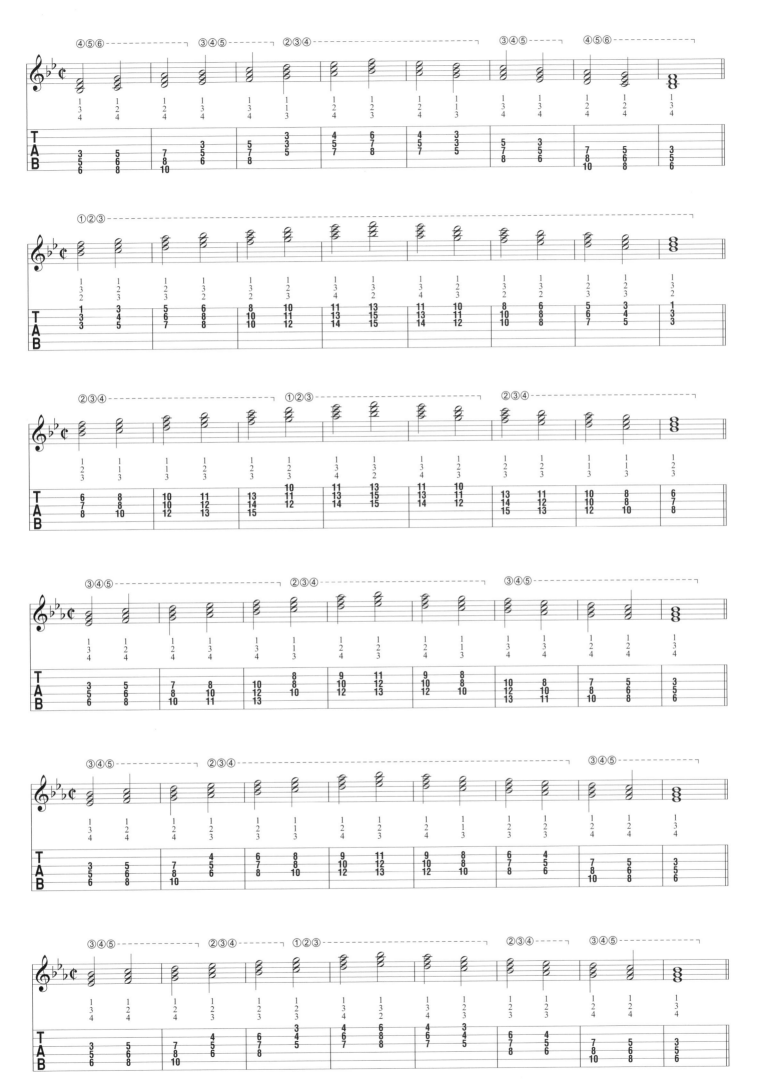

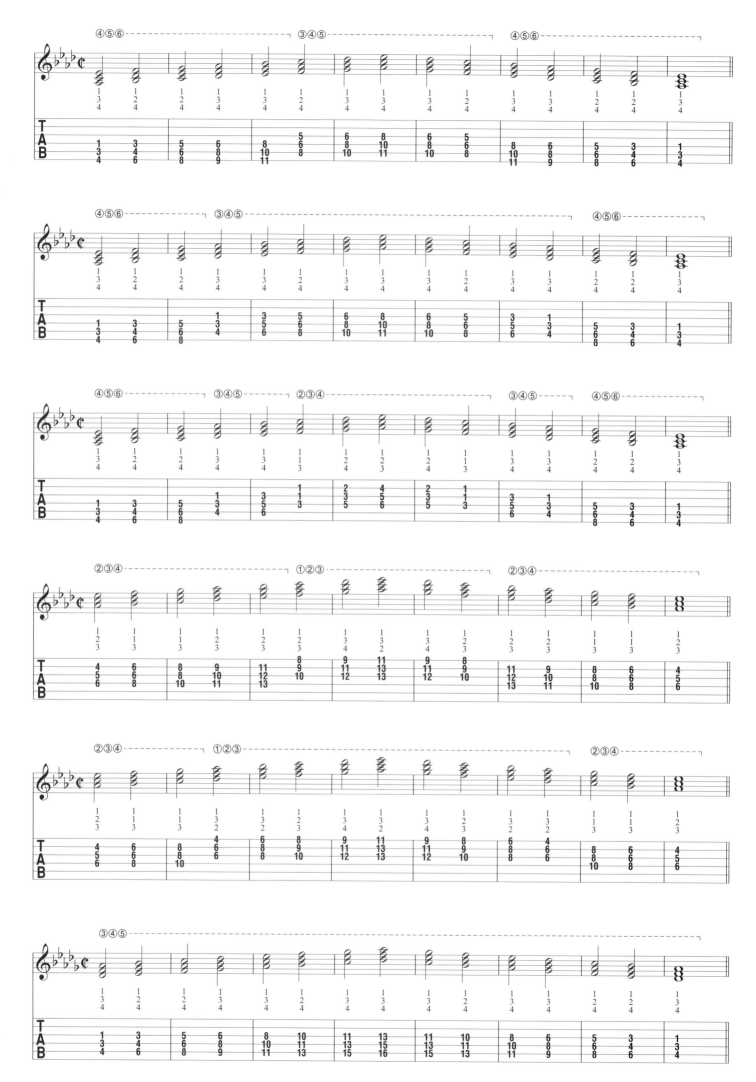

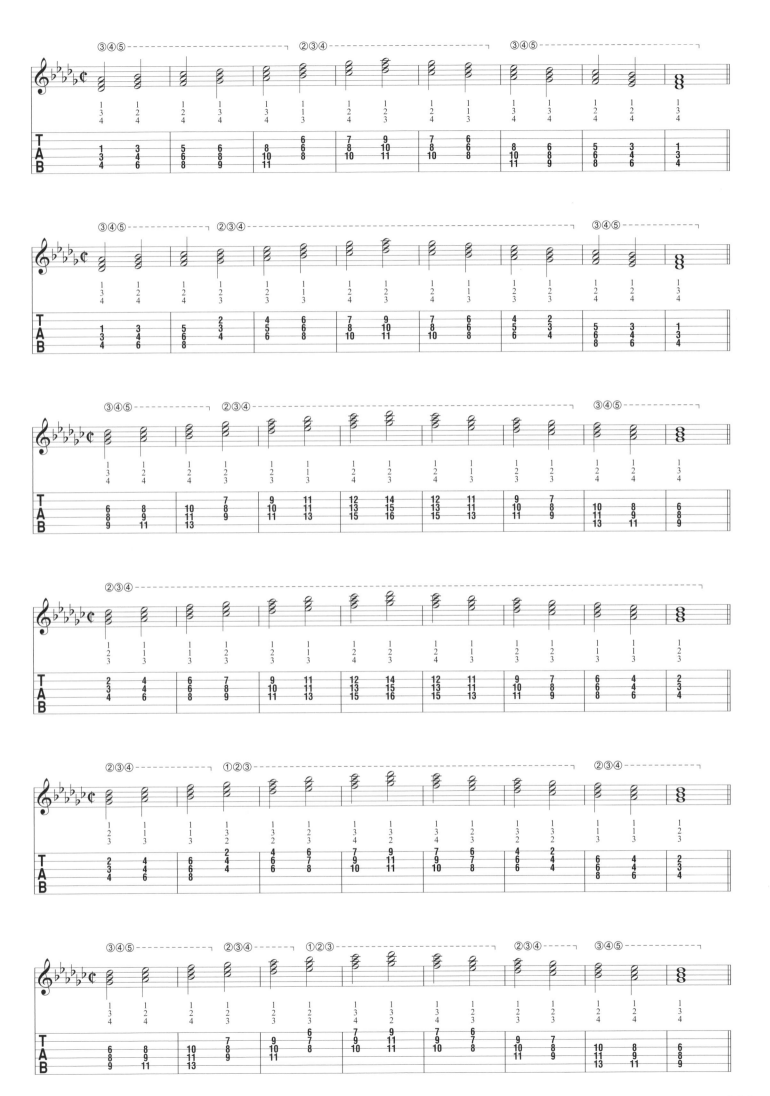

201

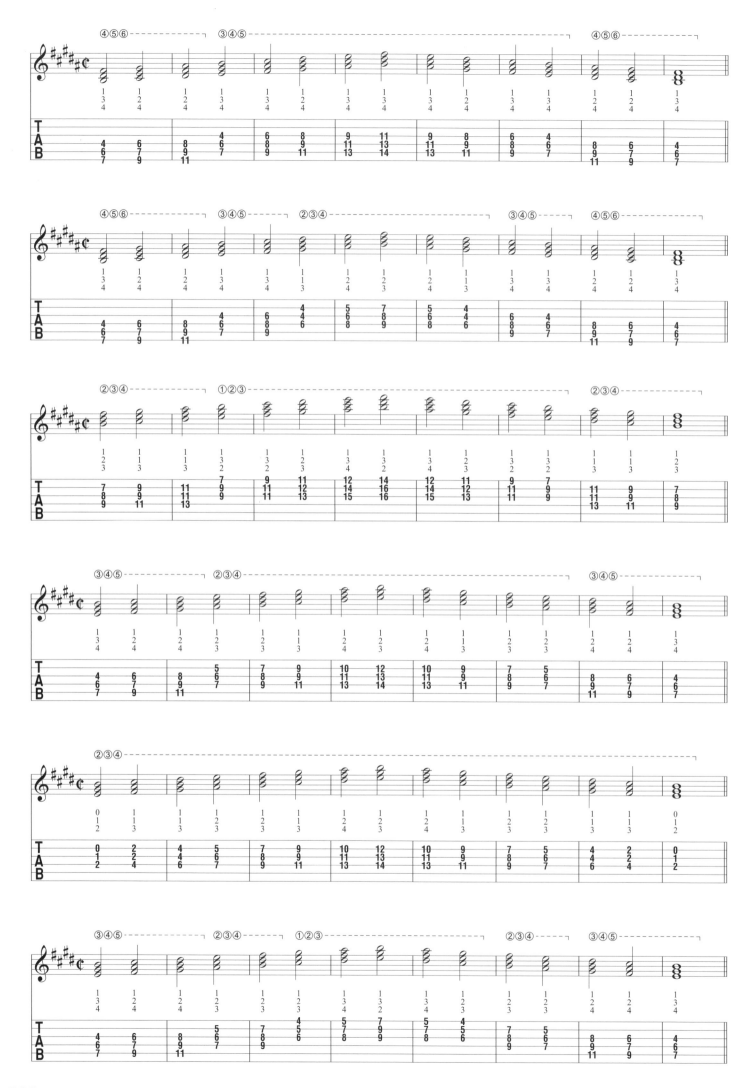

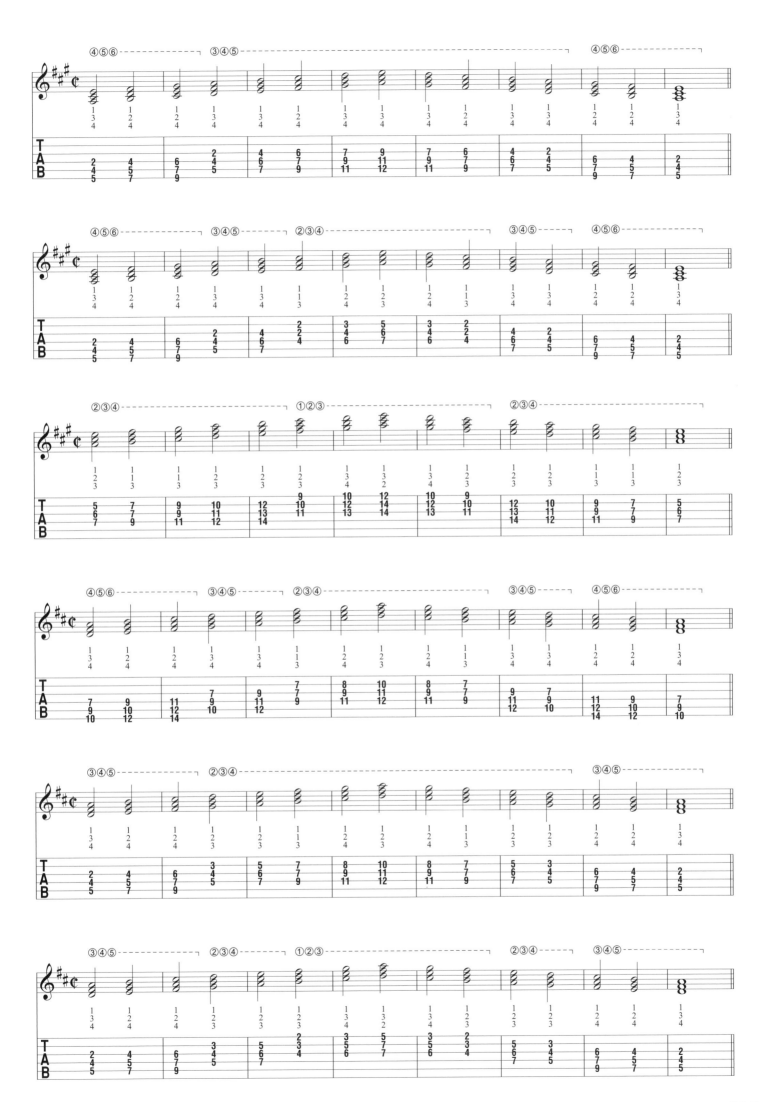

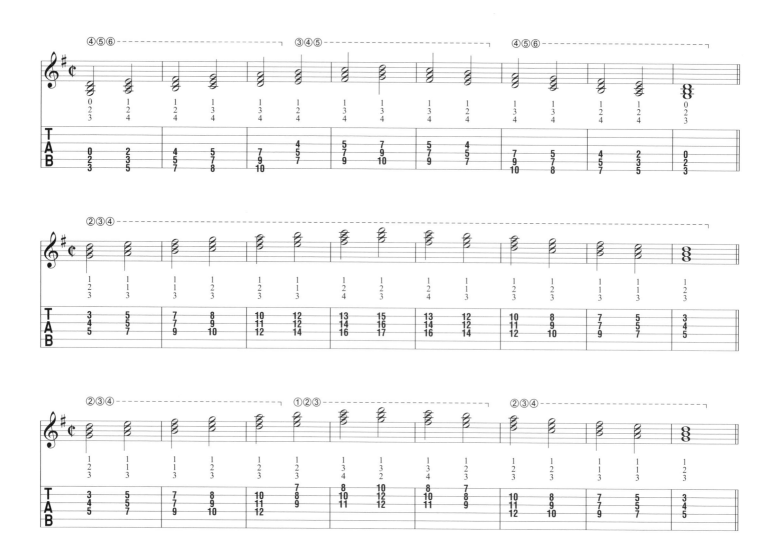

GUITAR NOTATION LEGEND

Guitar music can be notated three different ways: on a *musical staff*, in *tablature*, and in *rhythm slashes*.

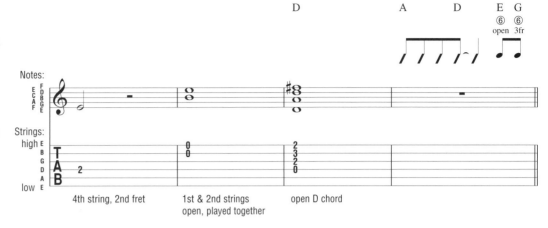

RHYTHM SLASHES are written above the staff. Strum chords in the rhythm indicated. Use the chord diagrams found at the top of the first page of the transcription for the appropriate chord voicings. Round noteheads indicate single notes.

THE MUSICAL STAFF shows pitches and rhythms and is divided by bar lines into measures. Pitches are named after the first seven letters of the alphabet.

TABLATURE graphically represents the guitar fingerboard. Each horizontal line represents a string, and each number represents a fret.

4th string, 2nd fret | 1st & 2nd strings open, played together | open D chord

Definitions for Special Guitar Notation

HALF-STEP BEND: Strike the note and bend up 1/2 step.

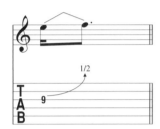

WHOLE-STEP BEND: Strike the note and bend up one step.

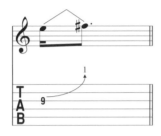

GRACE NOTE BEND: Strike the note and immediately bend up as indicated.

SLIGHT (MICROTONE) BEND: Strike the note and bend up 1/4 step.

BEND AND RELEASE: Strike the note and bend up as indicated, then release back to the original note. Only the first note is struck.

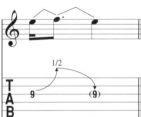

PRE-BEND: Bend the note as indicated, then strike it.

PRE-BEND AND RELEASE: Bend the note as indicated. Strike it and release the bend back to the original note.

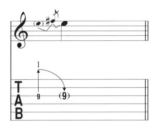

UNISON BEND: Strike the two notes simultaneously and bend the lower note up to the pitch of the higher.

VIBRATO: The string is vibrated by rapidly bending and releasing the note with the fretting hand.

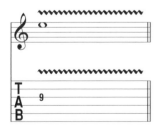

WIDE VIBRATO: The pitch is varied to a greater degree by vibrating with the fretting hand.

HAMMER-ON: Strike the first (lower) note with one finger, then sound the higher note (on the same string) with another finger by fretting it without picking.

PULL-OFF: Place both fingers on the notes to be sounded. Strike the first note and without picking, pull the finger off to sound the second (lower) note.

LEGATO SLIDE: Strike the first note and then slide the same fret-hand finger up or down to the second note. The second note is not struck.

SHIFT SLIDE: Same as legato slide, except the second note is struck.

TRILL: Very rapidly alternate between the notes indicated by continuously hammering on and pulling off.

TAPPING: Hammer ("tap") the fret indicated with the pick-hand index or middle finger and pull off to the note fretted by the fret hand.

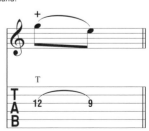

NATURAL HARMONIC: Strike the note while the fret-hand lightly touches the string directly over the fret indicated.

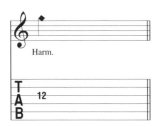

PINCH HARMONIC: The note is fretted normally and a harmonic is produced by adding the edge of the thumb or the tip of the index finger of the pick hand to the normal pick attack.

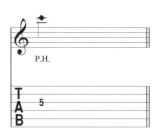

HARP HARMONIC: The note is fretted normally and a harmonic is produced by gently resting the pick hand's index finger directly above the indicated fret (in parentheses) while the pick hand's thumb or pick assists by plucking the appropriate string.

PICK SCRAPE: The edge of the pick is rubbed down (or up) the string, producing a scratchy sound.

MUFFLED STRINGS: A percussive sound is produced by laying the fret hand across the string(s) without depressing, and striking them with the pick hand.

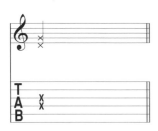

PALM MUTING: The note is partially muted by the pick hand lightly touching the string(s) just before the bridge.

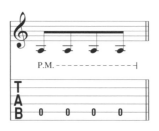

RAKE: Drag the pick across the strings indicated with a single motion.

TREMOLO PICKING: The note is picked as rapidly and continuously as possible.

ARPEGGIATE: Play the notes of the chord indicated by quickly rolling them from bottom to top.

VIBRATO BAR DIVE AND RETURN: The pitch of the note or chord is dropped a specified number of steps (in rhythm), then returned to the original pitch.

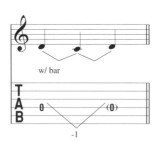

VIBRATO BAR SCOOP: Depress the bar just before striking the note, then quickly release the bar.

VIBRATO BAR DIP: Strike the note and then immediately drop a specified number of steps, then release back to the original pitch.

Additional Musical Definitions

 *(accent)* • Accentuate note (play it louder).

 *(accent)* • Accentuate note with great intensity.

 (staccato) • Play the note short.

 • Downstroke

V • Upstroke

D.S. al Coda • Go back to the sign (𝄋), then play until the measure marked "*To Coda*," then skip to the section labelled "**Coda**."

D.C. al Fine • Go back to the beginning of the song and play until the measure marked "*Fine*" (end).

Rhy. Fig. • Label used to recall a recurring accompaniment pattern (usually chordal).

Riff • Label used to recall composed, melodic lines (usually single notes) which recur.

Fill • Label used to identify a brief melodic figure which is to be inserted into the arrangement.

Rhy. Fill • A chordal version of a Fill.

tacet • Instrument is silent (drops out).

 • Repeat measures between signs.

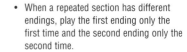 • When a repeated section has different endings, play the first ending only the first time and the second ending only the second time.

NOTE: Tablature numbers in parentheses mean:
1. The note is being sustained over a system (note in standard notation is tied), or
2. The note is sustained, but a new articulation (such as a hammer-on, pull-off, slide or vibrato) begins, or
3. The note is a barely audible "ghost" note (note in standard notation is also in parentheses).

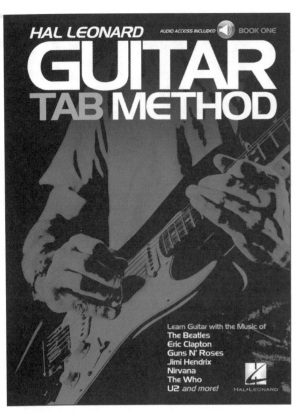

HAL LEONARD GUITAR TAB METHOD

Learn single notes with riffs like "Day Tripper" and "Crazy Train," power chords with classics by AC/DC and the Who, strumming with songs from Neil Young and Nirvana, and much more. Book 1 includes: parts of the guitar, easy-to-follow guitar tablature, notes & riffs starting on the low E string, tempo & time signatures, understanding notes and rests, palm muting, vibrato, power chords, open chords, strumming, slides and slurs, hammer-ons and pull-offs, many music styles, nearly 100 riffs and songs, online audio demos of every example, and more!
00697411 Book/Online Audio $12.99

BOOK 2

This innovative method for acoustic or electric guitar picks up where Book One leaves off. Learn notes up the fretboard with riffs like "Purple Haze" and "Sunshine of Your Love," lead guitar licks from Stevie Ray Vaughan and Eric Clapton, more chords with songs by the Beatles and Bob Dylan, and much more. The accompanying online audio access, available using the unique code in the book, features demos of all 80 riffs and songs in the book.
00696616 Book/Online Audio $12.99

BOOKS 1 & 2 COMBO EDITION

00696633 Book/Online Audio $24.99

BOOK 3

Book 3 includes: easy-to-follow guitar tablature; barre chords; minor scale; relative minor; Nashville numbering system; 12-bar blues; blues scale; blues licks & turnarounds; 12/8 time; add and sus chords; minor seventh chords; minor blues; variety of music styles; nearly 80 riffs and songs; audio demos of every example; and much more.
00126952 Book/Online Audio $12.99

SONGBOOK 1

Here are 10 hit songs tabbed for beginning guitarists to play while they are working through the Hal Leonard Guitar Tab Method, or any other guitar method. The CD features both examples of how the guitar should sound, and full-band backing tracks so students can play the lead! Songs: All the Small Things • Breaking the Law • Californication • Come Together • Free Fallin' • Lick It Up • Pork and Beans • Smells like Teen Spirit • 21 Guns • You Really Got Me.
00696604 Book/CD Pack $12.99

SONGBOOK 2

Here are 10 more hit songs to play while working through the Hal Leonard Guitar Tab Method: Born under a Bad Sign • Brain Stew • Fortunate Son • I Won't Back Down • Lithium • Mr. Jones • Rebel 'Rouser • Rolling in the Deep • Use Somebody • The Zoo.
00696655 Book/CD Pack $12.99

HAL LEONARD GUITAR TAB METHOD

THE FIRST AND ONLY BEGINNING GUITAR METHOD OF ITS KIND!

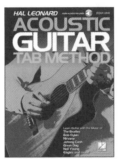

HAL LEONARD ACOUSTIC GUITAR TAB METHOD BOOK 1

Learn chords with songs like "Eleanor Rigby" and "Knockin' on Heaven's Door," single notes with riffs and solos by Nirvana and Pink Floyd, arpeggios with classics by Eric Clapton and Boston, and much more. Book 1 includes: parts of the guitar, easy-to-follow guitar tablature, notes & riffs starting on the low E string, tempo & time signatures, strumming patterns and arpeggios, slides and slurs, hammer-ons and pull-offs, many music styles, nearly 100 riffs and songs, audio demos of every example, and more!
00124197 Book/Online Audio $12.99

BOOK 2

Book Two also includes: easy-to-follow tablature; fingerpicking; sixteenth notes; triplets; major scale; basic music theory; the minor pentatonic scale; add and sus chords; lead licks; Travis picking; 6/8 time; using a capo; and more! Also includes nearly 80 riffs and songs with online audio demos of every example.
00131207 Book/Online Audio $12.99

HAL LEONARD LEFT-HANDED BASS TAB METHOD BOOK 1

by Eric W. Wills

Now left-handed players can learn everything there is to know about beginning bass guitar with riffs like "Day Tripper," "Billie Jean," and "With or Without You." Book 1 includes: parts of the bass, easy-to-follow tablature, notes & riffs starting on the low E string, tempo & time signatures, understanding notes and rests, proper fingering and technique, slides and slurs, hammer-ons and pull-offs, many music styles, nearly 100 riffs and songs, audio CD with demos of every example, and more!
00151140 Book/Online Audio $12.99

HAL LEONARD BASS TAB METHOD

by Eric W. Wills

Learn everything there is to know about beginning bass guitar with riffs like "Day Tripper," "Billie Jean," and "With or Without You." Book 1 includes: parts of the bass, easy-to-follow tablature, notes & riffs starting on the low E string, tempo & time signatures, understanding notes and rests, proper fingering and technique, slides and slurs, hammer-ons and pull-offs, many music styles, nearly 100 riffs and songs, audio CD with demos of every example, and more!
00113068 Book/CD Pack.. $12.99

BOOK 2

This innovative method for electric bass guitar picks up where Book One leaves off. Learn notes up the fretboard with riffs like "Sunshine of Your Love" and "Sweet Emotion," scales with songs by Ozzy Osbourne and R.E.M., beginning slap technique with songs like "Panic Station" and "Higher Ground," and much more. The accompanying online audio features demos of all 69 riffs and songs in the book.
00124754 Book/Online Audio $12.99

SONGBOOK 1

Here are 10 hit songs tabbed for beginning guitarists to play while they are working through the Hal Leonard Bass Tab Method, or any other method. The songs are all on facing pages for no page turns, and the CD features both examples of how the guitar should sound, and full-band backing tracks so students can play the lead! The songs include: Beverly Hills • Born Under a Bad Sign • Brown Eyed Girl • Crazy Train • Hey Joe • I Won't Back Down • Smoke on the Water • Stir It Up • Use Somebody • You Are the Sunshine of My Life.
00120236 Book/CD Pack.. $12.99

7777 W. BLUEMOUND RD. P.O. BOX 13819 MILWAUKEE, WI 53213
www.halleonard.com
Prices, contents, and availability subject to change without notice.

0416

IMPROVE YOUR IMPROV
AND OTHER JAZZ TECHNIQUES WITH BOOKS FROM HAL LEONARD

JAZZ GUITAR
HAL LEONARD GUITAR METHOD
by Jeff Schroedl

The Hal Leonard Jazz Guitar Method is your complete guide to learning jazz guitar. This book uses real jazz songs to teach the basics of accompanying and improvising jazz guitar in the style of Wes Montgomery, Joe Pass, Tal Farlow, Charlie Christian, Pat Martino, Barney Kessel, Jim Hall, and many others.
00695359 Book/Online Audio $19.99

AMAZING PHRASING
50 WAYS TO IMPROVE YOUR
IMPROVISATIONAL SKILLS • *by Tom Kolb*

This book/CD pack explores all the main components necessary for crafting well-balanced rhythmic and melodic phrases. It also explains how these phrases are put together to form cohesive solos. Many styles are covered – rock, blues, jazz, fusion, country, Latin, funk and more – and all of the concepts are backed up with musical examples.
00695583 Book/CD Pack............................ $19.95

BEST OF JAZZ GUITAR
by Wolf Marshall • Signature Licks

In this book/CD pack, Wolf Marshall provides a hands-on analysis of 10 of the most frequently played tunes in the jazz genre, as played by the leading guitarists of all time. Each selection includes technical analysis and performance notes, biographical sketches, and authentic matching audio with backing tracks.
00695586 Book/CD Pack............................ $24.95

CHORD-MELODY
PHRASES FOR GUITAR
by Ron Eschete • REH ProLessons Series

Expand your chord-melody chops with these outstanding jazz phrases! This book covers: chord substitutions, chromatic movements, contrary motion, pedal tones, inner-voice movements, reharmonization techniques, and much more. Includes standard notation and tab, and a CD.
00695628 Book/CD Pack............................ $17.99

CHORDS FOR JAZZ GUITAR
THE COMPLETE GUIDE TO COMPING,
CHORD MELODY AND CHORD SOLOING • *by Charlton Johnson*

This book/CD pack will teach you how to play jazz chords all over the fretboard in a variety of styles and progressions. It covers: voicings, progressions, jazz chord theory, comping, chord melody, chord soloing, voice leading and many more topics. The CD includes 98 full-band demo tracks. No tablature.
00695706 Book/CD Pack............................ $19.95

FRETBOARD ROADMAPS –
JAZZ GUITAR
THE ESSENTIAL GUITAR PATTERNS
THAT ALL THE PROS KNOW AND USE • *by Fred Sokolow*

This book/CD pack will get guitarists playing lead & rhythm anywhere on the fretboard, in any key! It teaches a variety of lead guitar styles using moveable patterns, double-note licks, sliding pentatonics and more, through easy-to-follow diagrams and instructions. The CD includes 54 full-demo tracks.
00695354 Book/CD Pack............................ $14.95

JAZZ IMPROVISATION FOR GUITAR
by Les Wise • REH ProLessons Series

This book/CD will allow you to make the transition from playing disjointed scales and arpeggios to playing melodic jazz solos that maintain continuity and interest for the listener. Topics covered include: tension and resolution, major scale, melodic minor scale, and harmonic minor scale patterns, common licks and substitution techniques, creating altered tension, and more! Features standard notation and tab, and a CD.
00695657 Book/CD Pack............................ $16.95

JAZZ RHYTHM GUITAR
THE COMPLETE GUIDE
by Jack Grassel

This book/CD pack will help rhythm guitarists better understand: chord symbols and voicings, comping styles and patterns, equipment, accessories and set-up, the fingerboard, chord theory, and much more. The accompanying CD includes 74 full-band tracks.
00695654 Book/CD Pack............................ $19.95

JAZZ SOLOS FOR GUITAR
LEAD GUITAR IN THE STYLES OF TAL FARLOW,
BARNEY KESSEL, WES MONTGOMERY, JOE PASS, JOHNNY SMITH
by Les Wise

Examine the solo concepts of the masters with this book including phrase-by-phrase performance notes, tips on arpeggio substitution, scale substitution, tension and resolution, jazz-blues, chord soloing, and more. The CD includes full demonstration and rhythm-only tracks.
00695447 Book/CD Pack............................ $17.95

100 JAZZ LESSONS
Guitar Lesson Goldmine Series
by John Heussenstamm and Paul Silbergleit

Featuring 100 individual modules covering a giant array of topics, each lesson includes detailed instruction with playing examples presented in standard notation and tablature. You'll also get extremely useful tips, scale diagrams, and more to reinforce your learning experience, plus 2 full audio CDs featuring performance demos of all the examples in the book!
00696454 Book/2-CD Pack $24.99

101 MUST-KNOW JAZZ LICKS
A QUICK, EASY REFERENCE GUIDE
FOR ALL GUITARISTS • *by Wolf Marshall*

Here are 101 definitive licks, plus demonstration audio, from every major jazz guitar style, neatly organized into easy-to-use categories. They're all here: swing and pre-bop, bebop, post-bop modern jazz, hard bop and cool jazz, modal jazz, soul jazz and postmodern jazz. Includes an introduction, tips, and a list of suggested recordings.
00695433 Book/Online Audio $17.99

SWING AND BIG BAND GUITAR
FOUR-TO-THE-BAR COMPING IN THE STYLE OF
FREDDIE GREEN • *by Charlton Johnson*

This unique package teaches the essentials of swing and big band styles, including chord voicings, inversions, substitutions; time and groove, reading charts, chord reduction, and expansion; sample songs, patterns, progressions, and exercises; chord reference library; and a CD with over 50 full-demo examples. Uses chord grids – no tablature.
00695147 Book/CD Pack............................ $19.99

Prices, contents and availability subject to change without notice.